MW01292802

School of the Woods

"THERE AT A TURN IN THE PATH, NOT TEN YARDS
AHEAD, STOOD A HUGE BEAR."

SCHOOL OF THE WOODS

Some Life Studies of Animal Instincts and Animal Training 🐇 🐇 🐇 By

WILLIAM J. LONG

Author of BEASTS OF THE FIELD
FOWLS OF THE AIR
WOOD FOLK SERIES
ETC.

ILLUSTRATED BY

CHARLES COPELAND

Yesterday's Classics

Cover and arrangement
© 2006 Yesterday's Classics.

This edition, first published in 2006 by Yesterday's Classics, is an unabridged republication of the work originally published by Ginn and Company in 1902. For a complete listing of books published by Yesterday's Classics, visit www.yesterdaysclassics.com. Yesterday's Classics is the publishing arm of the Baldwin Project which presents the complete text of dozens of classic books for children at www.mainlesson.com under the editorship of Lisa M. Ripperton and T. A. Roth.

ISBN-10:   1-59915-190-1

ISBN-13:   978-1-59915-190-8

Yesterday's Classics
PO Box 3418
Chapel Hill, NC 27515

To the gentle Brotherhood
of Nature Lovers
I dedicate this book of
Nature and Animal Life

Preface

MOST of the following sketches were made in the woods, with the subjects themselves living just outside my tent door. They are all life studies, and include also some of the unusual life secrets of a score of animals and birds, — shy, wild creatures, mostly, that hide from the face of man and make their nests or their lairs deep in the heart of the wilderness.

So far as the sketches have any unity, they are the result of an effort on the part of the writer to get at the heart of things and find

(Preface

the meaning of certain puzzling ways of birds and beasts. A suggestion, at least, of that meaning, and also an indication of the scope and object of this book, will be found in the first chapter, the Introduction to the " School of the Woods."

As in previous volumes, the names herein used for birds and animals are those given by the Milicete Indians. I use these names partly for their happy memories; partly for the added touch of individuality which they give to every creature; but chiefly because they have the trick of bringing the animal himself before you by some sound or suggestion. When you call the little creature that lives under your doorstep, that eats your crumbs and that comes when you whistle certain tunes, a common Toad, the word means nothing. But when Simmo speaks of K'dunk the Fat One, I know something of what the interesting little creature says, and just how he looks.

Two or three of these studies have already appeared in various magazines. All the rest come direct from my old notebooks and wilderness records to these newer pages, where the skillful pencil of my friend Mr. Charles Copeland makes the animals live again and peep at me shyly from behind old mossy logs, or glide away into their leafy solitudes, halting, listening, looking back at me inquisitively —just as they did in the wilderness.

WILLIAM J. LONG.

Stamford, Conn.,
September, 1902.

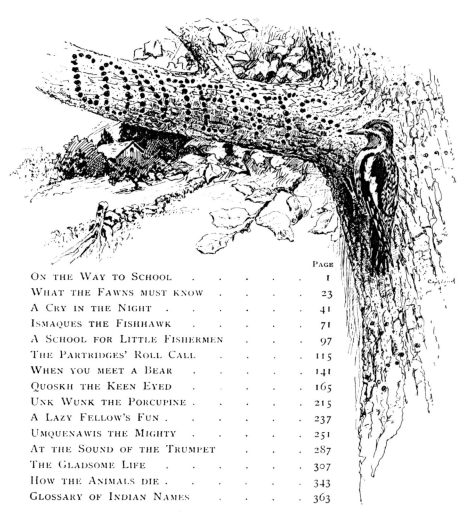

xi

Full Page Illustrations

xiii

On the Way to School

On The Way To School

MANY years ago the writer saw, for the second time, a mother otter teach her unsuspecting little ones to swim by carrying them on her back into the water, as if for a frolic, and there diving from under them before they realized what she was about. As they struggled wildly in the unknown element, she rose near them and began to help and encourage them on their erratic way back to the bank. When they reached it, at last, they scrambled out, whimpered, shook themselves, looked at

3

4
*On the Way
— to School*

the river fearfully, then glided into their den. Later they reappeared cautiously; but no amount of gentle persuasion on the mother's part could induce them to try for themselves another plunge into the water; nor, spite of her coaxing and playful rolling about in the dry leaves, would they climb again upon her back that day, as I had seen them and other young otters do, twenty times before, without hesitation.

Now to me, as I went home through the twilight woods thinking it all over, the most suggestive thing in the whole curious incident was this: that I had been taught 'to swim myself in exactly the same way by a bigger boy — with less of help and more of hilarity on his part, and a great deal more of splashing and sputtering on mine, than marked the progress of the young otters.

That interesting little comedy by the quiet river, one of the thousands that pass every day unnoticed in the summer woods, first opened my eyes to the fact that all wild creatures must learn most of what they know as we do; and to learn they must be taught. I have had that fact in mind in gathering together from my old notebooks and summer journals these sketches of animal life, which group themselves naturally about one central idea, namely, the large place which early education holds in the life of every creature.

5
On the Way to School —

That animal education is like our own, and so depends chiefly upon teaching, may possibly be a new suggestion in the field of natural history. Most people think that the life of a wild animal is governed wholly by instinct. They are of the same class who hold that the character of a child is largely predetermined by heredity.

Personally, after many years of watching animals in their native haunts, I am convinced that instinct plays a much smaller

part than we have supposed; that an animal's success or failure in the ceaseless struggle for life depends, not upon instinct, but upon the kind of training which the animal receives from its mother. And the more I see of children, the more sure am I that heredity (only another name for accumulated and developed instincts) plays but a small part in the child's history and destiny; that, instead, training — early training — is the chief factor; that Loyola, with a profound wisdom in matters childlike, such as the world has rarely seen, was right when he said, in substance: " Give me a child till he is seven years old, and it matters not much who has him afterwards. He is mine for time and eternity." Substitute seven weeks for seven years, and you have an inkling of the unconscious thought which governs every little mother in the wilderness.

To indicate the probable truth of this position, there are certain facts and traits of animal life which are open to even a casual observer in the woods and fields.

Those young birds and animals that are left by sad accident, or sadder willfulness, without their mothers' training profit little by their instincts. They are always first to fall in the battle with the strong. Those alone that follow their natural leaders till they learn wisdom live to grow up in the big woods. Sometimes, in the course of a long summer, birds and animals that see their first offspring well trained produce a second brood or litter. The latter are generally abandoned, at the approach of winter, before their simple education is half completed. Left with their instincts and their imperfect training, they go to feed nature's hungry prowlers; while the better trained broods live and thrive in the same woods, amid the same dangers. Moreover, domestic animals, which have all their wild instincts but none of the wild mother's

7
On the Way to School —

8

On the Way
— to School

training, far from profiting by their human association, are almost helpless when, by chance, they are lost or must take up the old, free life of the woods again. Instinct profits them nothing; they can neither catch their food nor hide from their enemies as well as their wilder kinsfolk, and they are the first to go down under the swoop or spring of hawk or wild-cat.

In a more specific way one may find the same idea suggested everywhere in the woods. I watched five or six mother caribou, one afternoon, teaching their little ones what seemed to me to be plain social regulations and rules of conduct. Up to that time the young had lived each one with its mother in lonely seclusion, as all wild creatures do,— an excellent plan, by the way, with a suggestion in it, possibly, for human mothers. Now they were brought together for the first time in preparation for their winter life on the barrens, when all caribou run in herds.

The mothers brought them to a natural opening in the woods, pushed them all out into the center by themselves, and left them to get acquainted — a slow, cautious process, with much shyness and wonder manifest on the part of the little caribou. Meanwhile the mothers watched over them from the shadows, encouraged the timid ones, and pushed apart or punished those that took to butting and bossing. Then, under guise of a frolic, they were taught to run in groups and to jump fallen trees, — a necessary but still a very difficult lesson for woodland caribou, whose home is now in the big woods, but whose muscles are so modified by previous centuries on the open Arctic plains that jumping is unnatural, and so must be taught with much care and patience.

Again, you find a little fawn hidden in the woods, as described in the next chapter, and are much surprised that, instead of running away, he comes to you fearlessly, licks your hand and follows you, calling wistfully, as you go away. You have yet to learn,

9

On the Way to School —

*On the Way
~to School*

perhaps, that fear is not instinctive; that most wild creatures, if found early, before they have been taught, have no fear, but only bright curiosity for one who approaches them gently.

A few weeks later, while prowling through the woods, you hear a sudden alarm blast, and see the same fawn bounding away as if for his life. You have not changed; your gentleness is the same, your heart as kind to every creature. What then has come over the son of Kish? Simply this: that one day, while the fawn was following his mother, a scent that was not of the woods stole in through the underbrush. At the first sniff the doe threw up her head, thrust her nose into the wind, snorted, and bounded away with a sharp call for the fawn to follow. Such a lesson rarely needs to be repeated. From that moment a certain scent means danger to the fawn, and when the friendly wind brings it to his

nostrils again he will bound away, as he was taught to do.   And of all deer that flee at our approach in the wilderness, not one in ten has ever seen a man or suffered any harm; they are simply obeying one of their early lessons.

There is a simpler way still, in which you may test the theory.   Find a crow's nest in the spring (I choose the crow because he is the wisest of birds, and his nest is not hard to find) and go there secretly when the young are almost ready to fly.   One day you will see the mother bird standing near the nest and stretching her wings over her little ones. Presently the young stand up and stretch their wings in imitation.   That is the first lesson.   Next day, perhaps, you will see the old bird lifting herself to tiptoe and holding herself there by vigorous flapping.   Again the young imitate, and soon learn that their wings are a power to sustain them.   Next day you may see both parent birds passing from branch to branch about the nest, aided by their wings in the long jumps.   The little

11

On the Way to School —

12

*On the Way
~ to School*

ones join the play, and lo! they have learned to fly without even knowing that they were being taught.

All this, of course, refers only to the higher forms of animal life, of which I am writing. The lower orders have no early training, simply because they need to know so little that instinct alone suffices. Each higher order, however, must know not only itself but all about the life below, on which it depends for food, and something of the life above, from which it must protect itself by speed or cunning; and there is no instinct sufficient for these things. Only a careful mother training can supply the lack, and make the little wild things ready for their battle with the world.

So far as I have observed, young fish receive no teaching whatever from their elders. Some of them follow the line of least resistance and go down stream to the sea. When the time for reproduction arrives they find their way back from the sea to the same river — always the same river — in which they were hatched. This double migration has been supposed to be purely a matter of instinct. I am not so sure. From studying trout and salmon particularly, and from recent records of deep-sea trawling, I think that, instead of following instinct, they follow the larger fishes from the same river, which are found in shoals at greater or less distances offshore.

This is certainly true of the birds. With them the instinct to migrate is a mere impulse, hardly more intelligent than that of rats and squirrels and frogs, all of which have, at times, the same strong tendency to migrate. Left to themselves, the young birds would never find their northern or southern homes; but with the impulse to move is another and stronger impulse, to go with the crowd. So the young birds join the migrating hosts, and from their wiser

13
On the Way to School —

14
On the Way
~ to School

elders, not from instinct, learn the sure way, down the coast and over the seas and through the unmapped wildernesses, to where food and quiet resting places are awaiting them.

The plovers are the only possible exception to this rule that I know. Young plovers start southward, over the immense reach from Labrador to Patagonia, some ten or twelve days earlier than their elders; but I have sometimes noticed, in a great flock of "pale-bellies" that a sudden southeaster had driven to a landing on our shores, two or three old "black-breasts"; and I have no doubt that these older birds are the guides, just as they seem to give the orders in the endless wing drills that plover practice as regularly as a platoon of soldiers.

Among the higher orders one can tread his ground more firmly. There, as with children, the first and strongest instinct of every creature is that of obedience. The essential difference between the two, between the human and the little wild animal, is this: the animal's one idea, born in him and strengthened by every day's training, is that, until he grows up and learns to take care of himself, his one business in the world is to be watchful for orders and to obey them instantly; while the child, by endless pettings and indulgences, by having every little cry attended to and fussed over as if it were a Cæsar's mandate, too often loses the saving instinct of obedience and grows up into the idea that his business in the world is to give orders for others to obey. So that at three or five or twenty years, when the mischief is done, we must begin to teach the obedience which should never have been lost, and without which life is a worse than useless thing.

When one turns to the animals, it is often with the wholesome, refreshing sense that here is a realm where the law of life is known and obeyed. To the wild creature obedience is everything. It is the deep, unconscious tribute of ignorance to wisdom, of weakness to power. All the wilderness mothers, from partridge to panther,

15

On the Way to School —

16

On the Way — to School

seize upon this and through long summer days and quiet starlit nights train and train it, till the young, profiting by their instinct of obedience, grow wise and strong by careful teaching. This, in a word, seems to me to be the whole secret of animal life. And one who watches the process with sympathetic eyes — this mother fishhawk, overcoming the young birds' natural instinct for hunting the woods, and teaching them the better mysteries of going a-fishing; this mother otter, teaching her young their first confidence in the water, which they naturally distrust, and then how to swim deep and silent — can only wonder and grow thoughtful, and mend his crude theories of instinct and heredity by what he sees, with open eyes, going on in the world all about him.

Therefore have I called this book the "School of the Woods"; for the summer wilderness is just one vast schoolhouse, of many rooms, in which a multitude of wise, patient mothers are teaching their little ones,

and of which our kindergartens are crude and second-rate imitations. Here are practical schools, technical schools. No superficial polish of French or literature will do here. Obedience is life; that is the first great lesson. Pity we men have not learned it better! Every wild mother knows it, lives by it, hammers it into her little ones. And then come other, secondary lessons, — when to hide and when to run; how to swoop and how to strike; how to sift and remember the many sights and sounds and smells of the world, and to suit action always and instantaneously to knowledge, — all of which, I repeat, are not so much matters of instinct as of careful training and imitation.

Life itself is the issue at stake in this forest education; therefore is the discipline stern as death. One who watches long over any of the wood-folk broods must catch his breath at times at the savage earnestness underlying even the simplest lesson. Few wild mothers will tolerate any trifling or willfulness in their little schools; and the more

17
On the Way to School —

**On the Way
— to School**

intelligent, like the crows and wolves, mercilessly kill their weak and wayward pupils. Yet tenderness and patience are here too, and the young are never driven beyond their powers. Once they have learned their lessons they are watched over for a few days by their teachers, and are then sent out into the world to put their education to the practical test of getting a living and of keeping alive.

One thing more: these interesting little wild kindergartens are, emphatically, happy gatherings. The more I watch them, teachers and pupils, the more I long for some measure of their freedom, their strength of play, their joyfulness. This is the great lesson which a man soon learns, with open eyes and heart, in the school of the woods.

There is a meadow lark out yonder — I watched him for half an hour yesterday — lying flat in the brown grass, his color hiding him from the great hawk that circles and circles overhead. Long ago that lark's mother taught him the wisdom of lying still. Now his one thought, so far as I can judge it, is how perfectly color and quietness hide him from those keen eyes that he has escaped so often. Ninety-nine times out of a hundred they do hide him perfectly, and he goes his way rejoicing. If he had any conception of Nature (which he has not), he would give thanks for his wonderful color and for the fact that Nature, when she gave the hawk keen eyes, remembered her other little children, and so made those eyes incapable of seeing a thing unless it moves or has conspicuous coloring. As it is, the lark thinks he did it all himself and rejoices in himself, as every other wild creature does.

19

On the Way to School —

20

On the Way
~to School

There can be no greater mistake, therefore, than to imagine an animal's life to be full of frightful alarms and haunting terrors. There is no terror in extreme watchfulness. To the animal it is simply the use of his unusual powers, with the joy and confidence that the use of unusual powers always brings, to animals as well as men. The eagle watching for prey far above his high mountain top has not more, but rather less, joy in his vision than the doe has in hers, who sees his sudden slanting flight and, knowing its meaning, hides her fawns and bids them lie still; while she runs away in plain sight, to take the robber's attention away from her little ones, and jumps for thick cover, at last, where the eagle's broad wings cannot follow. And she is not terrified, but glad as a linnet and exultant as a kingbird, when she comes cantering back again, after the danger is over.

Neither is there any terror, usually, but rather an exultant sense of power and victory in running away. Watch the deer, yonder, in his magnificent rush, light and swift as a hawk, over ground where other feet than his must halt and creep; watch the partridge in that clean, sure, curving plunge into the safety and shelter of the evergreen swamp. Hoof and wing alike seem to laugh at the danger behind, and to rejoice in their splendid power and training.

On the Way to School —

This simple fact, so glad in itself, so obvious to one who keeps his eyes open in Nature's world, is mentioned here by way of invitation — to assure the reader that, if he enter this school of the woods, he will see little truly of that which made his heart ache in his own sad world; no tragedies or footlight effects of woes and struggles, but rather a wholesome, cheerful life to make one glad and send him back to his own school with deeper wisdom and renewed courage.

Of late many letters have come to the writer from kindly, sympathetic people who are troubled at the thought of suffering, even of animal suffering. Some of them have also seen their children's tears at the imagined sorrows and woes of animals.

And these all ask: Is it true? do animals suffer, and sorrow in secret, and die tragically at the last?

It is partly in answer to these troubled questions that two chapters, of more general interest, are added to these studies of individual animals, instead of awaiting their place in a later volume of nature essays and addresses. They are The Gladsome Life and How the Animals Die. They sum up, in a general way, what seems to me to be the truth concerning animal life and death, as it appears to me now, after much watching and following the wild things of our woods and fields.

And now, if a too long introduction has not wearied the reader and kept his children waiting for animal stories, here is the school, and here are some of Nature's children that work and play therein.

What The Fawns Must Know

What the Fawns Must Know

O this day it is hard to understand how any eyes could have found them, they were so perfectly hidden. I was following a little brook, which led me by its singing to a deep dingle in the very heart of the big woods. A great fallen tree lay across my path and made a bridge over the stream. Now bridges are for crossing; that is plain to even the least of the wood folk; so I sat down on the mossy trunk to see who my neighbors might be, and what little feet were passing on the King's highway.

Here, beside me, are claw marks in the moldy bark. Only a bear could leave that deep, strong imprint. And see! there is where the moss slipped and broke beneath

What the Fawns Must Know

his weight. A restless tramp is Mooween, who scatters his records over forty miles of hillside on a summer day, when his lazy mood happens to leave him for a season. Here, on the other side, are the bronze-green petals of a spruce cone, chips from a squirrel's workshop, scattered as if Meeko had brushed them hastily from his yellow apron when he rushed out to see Mooween as he passed. There, beyond, is a mink sign, plain as daylight, where Cheokhes sat down a little while after his breakfast of frogs. And here, clinging to a stub, touching my elbow as I sit with heels dangling idly over the lazy brook, is a crinkly yellow hair, which tells me that Eleemos the Sly One, as Simmo calls him, hates to wet his feet, and so uses a fallen tree, or a stone in the brook, for a bridge, like his brother fox of the settlements.

Just in front of me was another fallen tree, lying alongside the stream in such a way that no animal more dangerous

than a roving mink would ever think of using it. Under its roots, away from the brook, was a hidden and roomy little house, with hemlock tips drooping over its doorway for a curtain. "A pretty place for a den," I thought; "for no one could ever find you there." Then, as if to contradict me, a stray sunbeam found the spot and sent curious bright glintings of sheen and shadow dancing and playing under the fallen roots and trunk. "Beautiful!" I cried, as the light fell on the brown mold and flecked it with white and yellow. The sunbeam went away again, but seemed to leave its brightness behind it; for there was still the gold-brown mold under the roots, and the flecks of white and yellow. I stooped down to see it better; I reached in my hand — then the brown mold changed suddenly to softest fur; the glintings of white and yellow were the dappled sides of two little fawns, lying there very still and frightened, just where their mother had hidden them when she went away.

27

What the Fawns Must Know

28

What the Fawns Must Know

They were but a few days old when I found them. Each had on his little Joseph's coat; and each, I think, must have had also a magic cloak somewhere about him; for he had only to lie down anywhere to become invisible. The curious markings, like the play of light and shadow through the leaves, hid the little owners perfectly, so long as they held themselves still and let the sunbeams dance over them. Their beautiful heads were a study for an artist, — delicate, graceful, exquisitely colored. And their great soft eyes had a questioning innocence, as they met yours, which went straight to your heart and made you claim the beautiful creatures for your own instantly. There is nothing in all the woods that so takes your heart by storm as the face of a little fawn.

They were timid at first, lying close, without motion of any kind. The instinct of obedience — the first and strongest instinct of every creature born into this world — kept them loyal to the mother's command to stay where they were and be still till she came back. So even after the hemlock curtain was brushed aside, and my eyes saw and my hand touched them, they kept their heads flat to the ground and pretended that they were only parts of the brown forest floor, and that the spots on their bright coats were but flecks of summer sunshine.

I felt then that I was an intruder; that I ought to go straight away and leave them; but the little things were too beautiful, lying there in their wonderful old den, with fear and wonder and questionings dancing in their soft eyes as they turned them back at me like a mischievous child playing peekaboo. It is a tribute to our higher nature that one cannot see a beautiful thing anywhere without wanting to draw near, to see, to touch, to possess it. And here was beauty such as one

29

What the Fawns Must Know

30

What the Fawns Must Know

rarely finds, and, though I was an intruder, I could not go away.

The hand that touched the little wild things brought no sense of danger with it. It searched out the spots behind their velvet ears, where they love to be rubbed; it wandered down over their backs with a little wavy caress in its motion; it curled its palm up softly under their moist muzzles and brought their tongues out instantly for the faint suggestion of salt that was in it. Suddenly their heads came up. Play was over now. They had forgotten their hiding, their first lesson; they turned and looked at me full with their great, innocent, questioning eyes. It was wonderful; I was undone. One must give his life, if need be, to defend the little things after they had looked at him just once like that.

When I rose at last, after petting them to my heart's content, they staggered up to their feet and came out of their house. Their mother had told them to stay; but here was another big kind animal, evidently, whom they might safely trust. "Take the gifts the gods provide thee" was the thought in their little heads; and the taste in their tongues' ends, when they licked my hand, was the nicest thing they had ever known. As I turned away they ran after me, with a plaintive little cry to bring me back. When I stopped they came close, nestling against me, one on either side, and lifted their heads to be petted and rubbed again.

31

What the Fawns Must Know

Standing so, all eagerness and wonder, they were a perfect study in first impressions of the world. Their ears had already caught the deer trick of twitching nervously and making trumpets at every sound. A leaf rustled, a twig broke, the brook's song swelled as a floating stick jammed in the current, and instantly the fawns were all alert. Eyes, ears, noses questioned the phenomenon. Then they would raise their eyes slowly to mine. "This is a wonderful world. This big wood is full of music. We know not. Tell us all about

32

What the Fawns Must Know

it," — that is what the beautiful eyes were saying as they lifted up to mine, full of innocence and delight at the joy of living. Then the hands that rested fondly, one on either soft neck, moved down from their ears with a caressing sweep and brought up under their moist muzzles. Instantly the wood and its music vanished; the questions ran away out of their eyes. Their eager tongues were out, and all the unknown sounds were forgotten in the new sensation of lapping a man's palm, with a wonderful taste hidden somewhere under its friendly roughnesses. They were still licking my hands, nestling close against me, when a twig snapped faintly far behind us.

Now twig snapping is the great index to all that passes in the wilderness. Curiously enough, no two animals can break even a twig under their feet and give the same warning. The *crack* under a bear's foot, except when he is stalking his game, is heavy and heedless. The hoof of a moose crushes a twig, and chokes the sound of it

before it can tell its message fairly. When a twig speaks under a deer in his passage through the woods, the sound is sharp, dainty, alert. It suggests the *plop* of a rain-drop into the lake. And the sound behind us now could not be mistaken. The mother of my little innocents was coming.

I hated to frighten her, and through her to destroy their new confidence; so I hurried back to the den, the little ones running close by my side. Ere I was halfway, a twig snapped sharply again; there was a swift rustle in the underbrush, and a doe sprang out, with a low bleat as she saw the home log. At sight of me she stopped short, trembling violently, her ears pointing forward like two accusing fingers, an awful fear in her soft eyes as she saw her little ones with her archenemy between them, his hands resting on their innocent necks. Her body swayed away, every muscle tense for the jump; but her feet seemed rooted to the spot. Slowly she swayed back to her balance, her eyes holding mine; then away again

34

What the Fawns Must Know

as the danger scent poured into her nose. But still the feet stayed. She could not move; could not believe. Then, as I waited quietly and tried to make my eyes say all sorts of friendly things, the harsh, throaty *K-a-a-a-h! k-a-a-a-h!* the danger cry of the deer, burst like a trumpet blast through the woods, and she leaped back to cover.

At the sound the little ones jumped as if stung, and plunged into the brush in the opposite direction. But the strange place frightened them; the hoarse cry that went crashing through the startled woods filled them with nameless dread. In a moment they were back again, nestling close against me, growing quiet as the hands stroked their sides without tremor or hurry.

Around us, out of sight, ran the fear-haunted mother, calling, calling; now showing her head, with the terror deep in her eyes; now dashing away, with her white flag up, to show her little ones the way they must take. But the fawns gave no heed after the first alarm. They felt the change; their ears were twitching nervously, and their eyes, which had not yet grown quick enough to measure distances and find their mother in her hiding, were full of strange terror as they questioned mine. Still, under the alarm, they felt the kindness which the poor mother, dog-driven and waylaid by guns, had never known. And they stayed, with a deep wisdom beyond all her cunning, where they knew they were safe.

I led them slowly back to their hiding place, gave them a last lick at my hands, and pushed them gently under the hemlock curtain. When they tried to come out I pushed them back again. "Stay there, and mind your mother; stay there, and follow your mother," I kept whispering. And to this day I have a half belief that they understood, not the word but the feeling behind it; for they grew quiet after a time and looked out with wide-open, wondering eyes. Then I dodged out of sight, jumped the fallen log, to throw them off the scent should

35
What the Fawns Must Know

What the Fawns Must Know

they come out, crossed the brook, and glided out of sight into the underbrush. Once safely out of hearing, I headed straight for the open, a few yards away, where the blasted white stems of the burned hillside showed through the green of the big woods, and climbed, and looked, and changed my position, till I could see the fallen tree under whose roots my little innocents were hiding.

The hoarse danger cry had ceased; the woods were all still again. A movement in the underbrush, and I saw the doe glide out beyond the brook and stand looking, listening. She bleated softly; the hemlock curtain was thrust aside, and the little ones came out. At sight of them she leaped forward, a great gladness showing eloquently in every line of her graceful body, rushed up to them, dropped her head and ran her keen nose over them, ears to tail and down their sides and back again, to be sure, and sure again, that they were her own little ones and were not harmed. All the while the

"THE WHITE FLAG SHOWING LIKE A BEACON
LIGHT AS SHE JUMPED AWAY"

fawns nestled close to her, as they had done a moment before to me, and lifted their heads to touch her sides with their noses, and ask in their own dumb way what it was all about, and why she had run away.

Then, as the smell of the man came to her from the tainted underbrush, the absolute necessity of teaching them their neglected second lesson, before another danger should find them, swept over her in a flood. She sprang aside with a great bound, and the hoarse *K-a-a-a-h ! k-a-a-a-h !* crashed through the woods again. Her tail was straight up, the white flag showing like a beacon light as she jumped away. Behind her the fawns stood startled a moment, trembling with a new wonder. Then their flags went up too, and they wabbled away on slender legs through the tangles and over the rough places of the wood, bravely following their leader. And I, watching from my hiding, with a vague regret that they could never again be mine, not even for a moment, saw only the crinkling lines of underbrush and

What the Fawns Must Know

here and there the flash of a little white flag. So they went up the hill and out of sight.

First, lie still; and second, follow the white flag. When I saw them again it needed no danger cry of the mother to remind them of these two things that every fawn must know who would live to grow up in the big woods.

A Cry In The Night

A Cry in the Night

THIS is the rest of the story, just as I saw it, of the little fawns that I found under the mossy log by the brook. There were two of them, you remember; and though they looked alike at first glance, I soon found out that there is just as much difference in fawns as there is in folks. Eyes, faces, dispositions, characters,—in all things they were as unlike as the virgins of the parable. One of them was wise, and the other was very foolish. The one was a follower, a learner; he never forgot his second lesson, to follow the white flag. The other followed from the first only his own willful head and feet, and discovered

43

44

A Cry in the Night

too late that obedience is life. Until the bear found him, I have no doubt he was thinking, in his own dumb, foolish way, that obedience is only for the weak and ignorant, and that government is only an unfair advantage which all the wilderness mothers take to keep little wild things from doing as they please.

The wise old mother took them both away when she knew I had found them, and hid them in a deeper solitude of the big woods, nearer the lake, where she could the sooner reach them from her feeding grounds. For days after the wonderful discovery I used to go in the early morning or the late afternoon, while mother deer are away feeding along the watercourses, and search the dingle from one end to the other, hoping to find the little ones again and win their confidence. But they were not there; and I took to watching instead a family of mink that lived in a den under a root, and a big owl that always slept in the same hemlock. Then, one day when a flock of partridges led me out of the wild

berry bushes into a cool green island of the burned lands, I ran plump upon the deer and her fawns lying all together under a fallen tree-top, dozing away the heat of the day.

They did not see me, but were only scared into action as a branch, upon which I stood looking for my partridges, gave way beneath my feet and let me down with a great crash under the fallen tree. There, looking out, I could see them perfectly, while Kookooskoos himself could hardly have seen me. At the first crack they all jumped like Jack-in-a-box when you touch his spring. The mother put up her white flag — which is the snowy under-side of her useful tail, and shows like a bea-con by day or night — and bounded away with a hoarse *Ka-a-a-a-h!* of warning. One of the little ones followed her on the instant, jumping squarely in his mother's tracks, his own little white flag flying to guide any that might come after him. But the second fawn ran off at a tangent, and stopped in a moment to stare and whistle and stamp his tiny foot in an odd mixture of curiosity and defiance.

The mother had to circle back twice before he followed her, at last, unwillingly. As she stole back each time, her tail was down and wiggling nervously — which is the sure sign, when you see it, that some scent of you is floating off through the woods and telling its warning into the deer's keen nostrils. But when she jumped away, the white flag was straight up, flashing in the very face of her foolish fawn, telling him as plain as any language what sign he must follow, if he would escape danger and avoid breaking his legs in the tangled underbrush.

I did not understand till long afterwards, when I had watched the fawns many times, how important is this latter suggestion. One who follows a frightened deer and sees or hears him go bounding off at breakneck pace over loose rocks and broken trees and tangled underbrush; rising swift on one side of a windfall without knowing what lies on the other side till he is already falling; driving like an arrow over ground where you must follow like a snail, lest you wrench a

foot or break an ankle, — finds himself asking
with unanswered wonder how any deer can
live half a season in the wilderness without
breaking all his legs. And when you run
upon a deer at night and hear him go smashing off in the darkness at the same reckless
speed, over a blow-down, perhaps, through
which you can barely force your way by daylight, then you realize suddenly that the most
wonderful part of a deer's education shows
itself, not in keen eyes or trumpet ears, or in
his finely trained nose, more sensitive a
hundred times than any barometer, but in
his forgotten feet, which seem to have eyes
and nerves and brains packed into their hard
shells, instead of the senseless matter you
see there.

Watch the doe yonder as she bounds away,
wigwagging her heedless little one to follow.
She is thinking only of him; and now you
see her feet free to take care of themselves.
As she rises over the big windfall, they
hang from the ankle joints, limp as a
glove out of which the hand has been

47
*A Cry in the
Night*

drawn, waiting and watching. One hoof touches a twig; like lightning it spreads and drops, after running for the smallest fraction of a second along the obstacle to know whether to relax or stiffen, or rise or fall to meet it. Just before she strikes the ground on the down plunge, see the wonderful hind hoofs sweep themselves forward, surveying the ground by touch, and bracing themselves, in a fraction of time so small that the eye cannot follow, for the shock of what lies beneath them, whether rock or rotten wood or yielding moss. The fore feet have followed the quick eyes above, and shoot straight and sure to their landing; but the hind hoofs must find the spot for themselves as they come down and, almost ere they find it, brace themselves again for the push of the mighty muscles above.

Once only I found where a fawn, with untrained feet, had broken its leg; and once I heard of a wounded buck, driven to death by dogs, that had fallen in the same way, never to rise again. Those were rare cases.

The marvel is that it does not happen to
every deer that fear drives through the
wilderness.

And that is another reason why the fawns
must learn to obey a wiser head than their
own. Till their little feet are educated, the
mother must choose the way for them; and
a wise fawn will jump squarely in her tracks.
That explains also why deer, even after they
are full grown, will often walk in single file,
a half-dozen of them sometimes following a
wise leader, stepping in his tracks and leaving but a single trail. It is partly, perhaps,
to fool their old enemy, the wolf, and their
new enemy, the man, by hiding the weakling's
trail in the stride and hoof mark of a big
buck; but it shows also the old habit, and
the training which begins when the fawns
first learn to follow the flag.

After that second discovery I used to go
in the afternoon sometimes to a point on
the lake nearest the fawns' hiding place, and
wait in my canoe for the mother to come out
and show me where she had left her little

ones. As they grew, and the drain upon her increased from their feeding, she seemed always half starved. Waiting in my canoe I would hear the crackle of brush, as she trotted straight down to the lake almost heedlessly, and see her plunge through the fringe of bushes that bordered the water. With scarcely a look or a sniff to be sure the coast was clear, she would jump for the lily pads. Sometimes the canoe was in plain sight; but she gave no heed as she tore up the juicy buds and stems, and swallowed them with the appetite of a famished wolf. Then I would paddle away and, taking my direction from her trail as she came, hunt diligently for the fawns until I found them.

This last happened only two or three times. The little ones were already wild; they had forgotten all about our first meeting, and when I showed myself, or cracked a twig too near them, they would promptly bolt into the brush. One always ran straight away, his white flag flying to show that he remembered his lesson; the other went off zigzag,

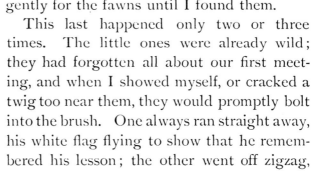

stopping at every angle of his run to look back and question me with his eyes and ears.

There was only one way in which such disobedience could end. I saw it plainly enough one afternoon, when, had I been one of the fierce prowlers of the wilderness, the little fellow's history would have stopped short under the paw of Upweekis, the shadowy lynx of the burned lands. It was late afternoon when I came over a ridge, following a deer path on my way to the lake, and looked down into a long narrow valley filled with berry bushes, and a few fire-blasted trees standing here and there to point out the perfect lone-liness and desolation of the place.

Just below me a deer was feeding hungrily, only her hind quarters showing out of the underbrush. I watched her awhile, then dropped on all fours and began to creep towards her, to see how near I could get and what new trait I might discover. But at the first motion (I had stood at first like an old stump on the ridge) a fawn that had evidently been watching me, among the bushes where

I could not see him, sprang into sight with a sharp whistle of warning. The doe threw up her head, looking straight at me, as if she had understood more from the signal than I had thought possible. There was not an instant's hesitation or searching. Her eyes went direct to me, as if the fawn's cry had said: " Behind you, mother, in the path by the second gray rock!" Then she jumped away, shooting up the opposite hill over roots and rocks as if thrown by steel springs, blowing hoarsely at every jump, and followed in splendid style by her watchful little one.

At the first snort of danger there was a rush in the underbrush near where she had stood, and a second fawn sprang into sight. I knew him instantly — the heedless one — and that he had neglected too long the matter of following the flag. He was confused, frightened, chuckle-headed now; he came darting up the deer path in the wrong direction, straight towards me, to within two jumps, before he noticed the man kneeling in the path before him and watching him quietly.

At the startling discovery he stopped short, seeming to shrink smaller and smaller before my eyes. Then he edged sidewise to a great stump, hid himself among the roots, and stood stock-still, — a beautiful picture of innocence and curiosity, framed in the rough brown roots of the spruce stump. It was his first teaching, to hide and be still. Just as he needed it most, he had forgotten absolutely the second lesson.

53
A Cry in the Night

We watched each other full five minutes without moving an eyelash. Then his first lesson ebbed away. He sidled out into the path again, came towards me two dainty, halting steps, and stamped prettily with his left fore foot. He was a young buck, and had that trick of stamping without any instruction. It is an old, old ruse to make you move, to startle you by the sound and threatening motion into showing who you are and what are your intentions.

But still the man did not move; the fawn grew frightened at his own boldness and ran away down the path. Far up the opposite

hill I heard the mother calling him. But he heeded not; he wanted to find out things for himself. There he was in the path again, watching me. I took out my handkerchief and waved it gently; at which great marvel he trotted back, stopping anon to look and stamp his little foot, to show me that he was not afraid.

"Brave little chap, I like you," I thought, my heart going out to him as he stood there with his soft eyes and beautiful face, stamping his little foot. "But what," my thoughts went on, "had happened to you ere now, had a bear or lucivee lifted his head over the ridge? Next month, alas! the law will be off; then there will be hunters in these woods, some of whom leave their hearts, with their wives and children, behind them. You can't trust them, believe me, little chap. Your mother is right; you can't trust them."

The night was coming swiftly. The mother's call, growing ever more anxious, more insistent, swept over the darkening hillside. "Perhaps," I thought, with sudden twinges and alarms of conscience, "perhaps I set you all wrong, little chap, in giving you the taste of salt that day, and teaching you to trust things that meet you in the wilderness." That is generally the way when we meddle with Mother Nature, who has her own good reasons for doing things as she does. " But no! there were two of you under the old log that day; and the other, — he's up there with his mother now, where you ought to be, — he knows that old laws are safer than new thoughts, especially new thoughts in the heads of foolish youngsters. You are all wrong, little chap, for all your pretty curiosity, and the stamp of your little foot that quite wins my heart. Perhaps I am to blame, after all; anyway, I'll teach you better now."

At the thought I picked up a large stone and sent it crashing, jumping, tearing down the hillside straight at him. All his bravado vanished like a wink. Up went his flag, and away he went over the logs and rocks of the great hillside; where presently I heard his mother running in a great circle till

55

A Cry in the Night

A Cry in the Night

she found him with her nose, thanks to the wood wires and the wind's message, and led him away out of danger.

One who lives for a few weeks in the wilderness, with eyes and ears open, soon finds that, instead of the lawlessness and blind chance which seem to hold sway there, he lives in the midst of law and order — an order of things much older than that to which he is accustomed, with which it is not well to interfere. I was uneasy, following the little deer path through the twilight stillness; and my uneasiness was not decreased when I found on a log, within fifty yards of the spot where the fawn first appeared, the signs of a big lucivee, with plenty of fawn's hair and fine-cracked bones to tell me what he had eaten for his midnight dinner.

Down at the lower end of the same deer path, where it stopped at the lake to let the wild things drink, was a little brook. Outside the mouth of this brook, among the rocks, was a deep pool; and in the pool lived some big trout. I was there one night, some two weeks later, trying to catch some of the big trout for my breakfast.

Those were wise fish. It was of no use to angle for them by day any more. They knew all the flies in my book; could tell the new Jenny Lind from the old Bumble Bee before it struck the water; and seemed to know perfectly, both by instinct and experience, that they were all frauds, which might as well be called Jenny Bee and Bumble Lind for any sweet reasonableness that was in them. Besides all this, the water was warm; the trout were logy and would not rise.

By night, however, the case was different. A few of the trout would leave the pool and prowl along the shores in shallow water, to see what tidbits the darkness might bring, in the shape of night bugs and careless piping frogs and sleepy minnows. Then, if you built a fire on the beach and cast a white-winged fly across the path of the firelight, you would sometimes get a big one.

It was fascinating sport always, whether the trout were rising or not. One had to fish with his ears, and keep most of his brains in his hand, ready to strike quick and hard when the moment came, after an hour of casting. Half the time you would not see your fish at all, but only hear the savage plunge as he swirled down with your fly. At other times, as you struck sharply at the plunge, your fly would come back to you, or tangle itself up in unseen snags; and far out, where the verge of the firelight rippled away into darkness, you would see a sharp wave-wedge shooting away; which told you that your trout was only a musquash. Swimming quietly by, he had seen you and your fire, and slapped his tail down hard on the water to make you jump. That is a way Musquash has in the night, so that he can make up his mind what queer thing you are and what you are doing.

All the while, as you fish, the great dark woods stand close about you, silent, listening. The air is full of scents and odors that steal abroad only by night, while the air is dew-laden. Strange cries, calls, squeaks, rustlings run along the hillside, or float in from the water, or drop down from the air overhead, to make you guess and wonder what wood folk are abroad at such unseemly hours, and what they are about. So that it is good to fish by night, as well as by day, and go home with heart and head full, even though your creel be empty.

I was standing very still by my fire, waiting for a big trout that had risen twice to regain his confidence, when I heard cautious rustlings in the brush behind me. I turned instantly, and there were two great glowing spots, the eyes of a deer, flashing out of the dark woods. A swift rustle, and two more coals glow lower down, flashing and scintillating with strange colors; and then two more; and I know that the doe and her fawns are there, stopped and fascinated on

their way to drink by the great wonder of the light and the dancing shadows, that rush up at timid wild things, as if to frighten them, but only jump over them and back again, as if inviting them to join the silent play.

I knelt down quietly beside my fire, slipping on a great roll of birch bark, which blazed up brightly, filling the woods with light. There, under a spruce, where a dark shadow had been a moment agone, stood the mother, her eyes all ablaze with the wonder of the light; now staring steadfastly into the fire; now starting nervously, with low questioning snorts, as a troop of shadows ran up to play hop-scotch with the little ones, who stood close behind her, one on either side.

A moment only it lasted. Then one fawn — I knew the heedless one, even in the fire-light, by his face and by his bright-dappled Joseph's coat — came straight towards me, stopping to stare with flashing eyes when the fire jumped up, and then to stamp his little foot at the shadows to show them that he was not afraid.

"HER EYES ALL ABLAZE WITH THE
WONDER OF THE LIGHT"

The mother called him anxiously; but still he came on, stamping prettily. She grew uneasy, trotting back and forth in a half circle, warning, calling, pleading. Then, as he came between her and the fire, and his little shadow stretched away up the hill where she was, showing how far away he was from her and how near the light, she broke away from its fascination with an immense effort: *Ka-a-a-h! ka-a-a-h!* the hoarse cry rang through the startled woods like a pistol shot; and she bounded away, her white flag shining like a wave crest in the night to guide her little ones.

The second fawn followed her instantly; but the heedless one barely swung his head to see where she was going, and then came on towards the light, staring and stamping in foolish wonder.

I watched him a little while, fascinated myself by his beauty, his dainty motions, his soft ears with a bright oval of light about them, his wonderful eyes glowing like burning rainbows, kindled by the firelight. Far

behind him the mother's cry ran back and forth along the hillside. Suddenly it changed; a danger note leaped into it; and again I heard the call to follow and the crash of brush as she leaped away. I remembered the lynx and the sad little history written on the log above. As the quickest way of saving the foolish youngster, I kicked my fire to pieces and walked out towards him. Then, as the wonder vanished in darkness and the scent of the man poured up to him on the lake's breath, the little fellow bounded away — alas! straight up the deer path, at right angles to the course his mother had taken a moment before.

Five minutes later I heard the mother calling a strange note in the direction he had taken, and went up the deer path very quietly to investigate. At the top of the ridge, where the path dropped away into a dark narrow valley with dense underbrush on either side, I heard the fawn answering her below me among the big trees, and knew instantly that something had happened. He called continuously, a plaintive cry of distress, in the black darkness of the spruces. The mother ran around him in a great circle, calling him to come; while he lay helpless in the same spot, telling her he could not, and that she must come to him. So the cries went back and forth in the listening night. — *Hoo-wuh*, "come here." *Bla-a-a, blr-r-t*, "I can't; come here." *Ka-a-a-h, ka-a-a-h!* "danger, follow!" — and then the crash of brush as she rushed away, followed by the second fawn; whom she must save, though she abandoned the heedless one to prowlers of the night.

It was clear enough what had happened. The cries of the wilderness have all their meaning, if one but knows how to interpret them. Running through the dark woods, his untrained feet had missed their landing, and he lay now under some rough windfall, with a broken leg to remind him of the lesson he had neglected so long.

I was stealing along towards him, feeling my way among the trees in the darkness, stopping every moment to listen to his cry

65

A Cry in the Night

66

A Cry in the Night

to guide me, when a heavy rustle came creeping down the hill and passed close before me. Something, perhaps, in the sound — a heavy though almost noiseless onward push, which only one creature in the woods can possibly make — something, perhaps, in a faint new odor in the moist air told me instantly that keener ears than mine had heard the cry; that Mooween the bear had left his blueberry patch, and was stalking the heedless fawn, whom he knew, by the hearing of his ears, to have become separated from his watchful mother in the darkness.

I regained the path silently — though Mooween heeds nothing when his game is afoot — and ran back to the canoe for my rifle. Ordinarily a bear is timid as a rabbit; but I had never met one so late at night before, and knew not how he would act should I take his game away. Besides, there is everything in the feeling with which one approaches an animal. If one comes timidly, doubtfully, the animal knows it; and if one comes swift, silent, resolute, with his power gripped tight, and the hammer back, and a forefinger resting lightly on the trigger guard, the animal knows it too you may depend. Anyway, they always act as if they knew; and you may safely follow the rule that, whatever your feeling is, whether fear or doubt or confidence, the large and dangerous animals will sense it instantly and adopt the opposite feeling for their rule of action. That is the way I have always found it in the wilderness. I met a bear once on a narrow path — but I must tell about that elsewhere.

The cries had ceased; the woods were all dark and silent when I came back. I went as swiftly as possible — without heed or caution; for whatever crackling I made the bear would attribute to the desperate mother — to the spot where I had turned back. Thence I went on cautiously, taking my bearings from one great tree on the ridge that lifted its bulk against the sky; slower and slower, till, just this side a great windfall, a twig cracked sharply under my foot. It was answered instantly by a grunt and a jump

67

A Cry in the Night

A Cry in the Night

beyond the windfall — and then the crashing rush of a bear up the hill, carrying something that caught and swished loudly on the bushes as it passed, till the sounds vanished in a faint rustle far away, and the woods were still again.

All night long, from my tent over beyond an arm of the big lake, I heard the mother calling at intervals. She seemed to be running back and forth along the ridge, above where the tragedy had occurred. Her nose told her of the bear and the man; but what awful thing they were doing with her little one she knew not. Fear and questioning were in the calls that floated down the ridge and across the water to my little tent.

At daylight I went back to the spot. I found without trouble where the fawn had fallen; the moss told mutely of his struggle; and a stain or two showed where Mooween grabbed him. The rest was a plain trail, of crushed moss and bent grass and stained leaves, and a tuft of soft hair here and there on the jagged ends of knots in the old

windfalls. So the trail hurried up the hill into a wild rough country, where it was of no use to follow.

As I climbed the last ridge on my way back to the lake, I heard rustlings in the underbrush, and then the unmistakable crack of a twig under a deer's foot. The mother had winded me; she was now following and circling down wind, to find out whether her lost fawn were with me. As yet she knew not what had happened. The bear had frightened her into extra care of the one fawn of whom she was sure. The other had simply vanished into the silence and mystery of the great woods.

Where the path turned downward, in sight of the lake, I saw her for a moment plainly, standing half hid in the underbrush, looking intently at my old canoe. She saw me at the same instant and bounded away, quartering up the hill in my direction. Near a thicket of evergreen that I had just passed, she sounded her hoarse *K-a-a-h, k-a-a-h!* and threw up her flag. There was a rush within the thicket; a sharp *k-a-a-h !* answered hers. Then the second fawn burst out of the cover where she had hidden him, and darted along the ridge after her, jumping like a big red fox from rock to rock, rising like a hawk over the windfalls, hitting her tracks wherever he could, and keeping his little nose hard down to his one needful lesson of following the white flag.

ISMAQUES THE FISHHAWK

ISMAQUES, THE FISHHAWK

Whit, *whit, ch'wee?* *Whit, whit, whit, ch'weeeee!* over my head went the shrill whistling, the hunting cry of Ismaques. Looking up from my fishing, I could see the broad wings sweeping over me, and catch the bright gleam of his eye as he looked down into my canoe, or behind me at the cold place among the rocks, to see if I were catching anything. Then, as he noted the pile of fish, — a blanket of silver on the black rocks, where I was stowing away chub for bear bait, — he would drop lower in amazement to see how I did it. When the trout were not rising, and his keen glance saw no gleam of red and gold in my canoe, he would circle off with a cheery *K'wee!* the good-luck call of a brother fisherman. For there is

73

74
**Ismaques
the Fishhawk**

no envy nor malice nor any uncharitableness in Ismaques. He lives in harmony with the world, and seems glad when you land a big one, though he is hungry himself, and the clamor from his nest, where his little ones are crying, is too keen for his heart's content.

What is there in going a-fishing, I wonder, that seems to change even the leopard's spots, and that puts a new heart into the man who hies him away to the brook when buds are swelling? There is Keeonekh the otter. Before he turned fisherman he was fierce, cruel, bloodthirsty, with a vile smell about him, like all the other weasels. Now he lives at peace with all the world and is clean, gentle, playful as a kitten and faithful as a dog when you make a pet of him. And there is Ismaques the fishhawk. Before he turned fisherman he was hated, like every other hawk, for his fierceness and his bandit ways. The shadow of his wings was the signal for hiding to all the timid ones. Jay and crow cried *Thief! thief!* and kingbird sounded his war cry and rushed out to battle. Now the little birds build their nests among the sticks of his great house, and the shadow of his wings is a sure protection. For owl and hawk and wild-cat have learned long since the wisdom of keeping well away from Ismaques' dwelling.

Not only the birds, but men also, feel the change in Ismaques' disposition. I hardly know a hunter who will not go out of his way for a shot at a hawk; but they send a hearty good-luck after this winged fisherman of the same fierce family, even though they see him rising heavily out of the very pool where the big trout live, and where they expect to cast their flies at sundown. Along the southern New England shores his coming — regular as the calendar itself — is hailed with delight by the fishermen. One state, at least, where he is most abundant, protects him by law; and even our Puritan forefathers, who seem to have neither made nor obeyed any game laws, looked upon him with a kindly eye, and made him an exception to the general license for killing. To their

76
*Ismaques
the Fishhawk*

credit, be it known, they once "publikly reeprimanded" one Master Eliphalet Bodman, a son of Belial evidently, for violently, with powder and shot, doing away with one fishhawk, and wickedly destroying the nest and eggs of another.

Whether this last were also done violently, with powder and shot, by blowing the nest to pieces with an old gun, or in simple boyfashion by shinning up the tree, the quaint old town record does not tell. But all this goes to show that our ancestors of the coast were kindly people at heart; that they looked upon this brave, simple fisherman, who built his nest by their doors, much as the German village people look upon the stork that builds upon their chimneys, and regarded his coming as an omen of good luck and plenty to the fisher folk.

Far back in the wilderness, where Ismaques builds his nest and goes a-fishing just as his ancestors did a thousand years ago, one finds the same honest bird, unspoiled alike by plenty or poverty, that excited our boyish

imagination and won the friendly regard of
our ancestors of the coast. Opposite my
camp on the lake, where I tarried long one
summer, charmed by the beauty of the place
and the good fishing, a pair of fishhawks
had built their nest in the top of a great
spruce on the mountain side. It was this
pair of birds that came daily to circle over
my canoe, or over the rocks where I fished
for chub, to see how I fared, and to send back
a cheery *Ch'wee! chip, ch'weeee!* "good luck
and good fishing," as they wheeled away. It
would take a good deal of argument now to
convince me that they did not at last recognize me as a fellow-fisherman, and were not
honestly interested in my methods and success.

At first I went to the nest, not so much
to study the fishhawks as to catch fleeting
glimpses of a shy, wild life of the woods, which
is hidden from most eyes. The fishing was
good, and both birds were expert fishermen.
While the young were growing, there was
always an abundance in the big nest on the
spruce top. The overflow of this abundance,

77
**Ismaques the
Fishhawk**

in the shape of heads, bones, and unwanted remnants, was cast over the sides of the nest and furnished savory pickings for a score of hungry prowlers. Mink came over from frog hunting in the brook, drawn by the good smell in the air. Skunks lumbered down from the hill, with a curious, hollow, bumping sound to announce their coming. Weasels, and one grizzly old pine marten, too slow or rheumatic for successful tree hunting, glided out of the underbrush and helped themselves without asking leave. Wild-cats quarreled like fiends over the pickings; more than once I heard them there screeching in the night. And one late afternoon, as I lingered in my hiding among the rocks while the shadows deepened, a big lucivee stole out of the bushes, as if ashamed of himself, and took to nosing daintily among the fish bones.

It was his first appearance, evidently. He did not know that the feast was free, but thought all the while that he was stealing somebody's catch. One could see it all in his attitudes, his starts and listenings, his low growlings to himself. He was bigger than anybody else there, and had no cause to be afraid; but there is a tremendous respect among all animals for the chase law and the rights of others; and the big cat felt it. He was hungry for fish; but, big as he was, his every movement showed that he was ready to take to his heels before the first little creature that should rise up and screech in his face: " This is mine ! " Later, when he grew accustomed to things and the fishhawks' generosity in providing a feast for all who might come in from the wilderness byways and hedges, he would come in boldly enough and claim his own ; but now, moving stealthily about, halting and listening timidly, he furnished a study in animal rights that repaid in itself all the long hours of watching.

But the hawks themselves were more interesting than their unbidden guests. Ismaques, honest fellow that he is, mates for life, and comes back to the same nest year after year. The only exception to this rule that I know, is in the case of a fishhawk, whom I knew well as a boy, and who lost his mate one summer by an accident. The accident came from a gun in the hands of an unthinking sportsman. The grief of Ismaques was evident, even to the unthinking. One could hear it in the lonely, questioning cry that he sent out over the still summer woods; and see it in the sweep of his wings as he went far afield to other ponds — not to fish, for Ismaques never fishes on his neighbor's preserves, but to search for his lost mate. For weeks he lingered in the old haunts, calling and searching everywhere; but at last the loneliness and the memories were too much for him. He left the place long before the time of migration had come; and the next spring a strange couple came to the spot, repaired the old nest, and went fishing in the pond. Ordinarily, the birds respect each other's fishing grounds, and especially the old nests; but this pair came and took possession without hesitation, as if they had some understanding with the former owner, who never came back again.

The old spruce on the mountain side had been occupied many years by my fishing friends. As is usually the case, it had given up its life to its bird masters. The oil from their frequent feastings had soaked into the bark, following down and down, checking the sap's rising, till at last it grew discouraged and ceased to climb. Then the tree died and gave up its branches, one by one, to repair the nest above. The jagged, broken ends showed everywhere how they had been broken off to supply the hawks' necessities.

There is a curious bit of building lore suggested by these broken branches, that one may learn for himself any springtime by watching the birds at their nest building. Large sticks are required for a foundation. The ground is strewed with such; but Ismaques never comes down to the ground if he can avoid it. Even when he drops an unusually heavy fish, in his flight above the trees, he looks after it regretfully, but never follows. He may be hungry, but he will not set his huge hooked talons on the earth.

Ismaques the Fishhawk

He cannot walk, and loses all his power there. So he goes off and fishes patiently, hours long, to replace his lost catch.

When he needs sticks for his nest, he searches out a tree and breaks off the dead branches by his weight. If the stick be stubborn, he rises far above it and drops like a cannon ball, gripping it in his claws and snapping it short off at the same instant by the force of his blow. Twice I have been guided to where Ismaques and his mate were collecting material by reports like pistol shots ringing through the wood, as the great birds fell upon the dead branches and snapped them off. Once, when he came down too hard, I saw him fall almost to the ground, flapping lustily, before he found his wings and sailed away with his four-foot stick triumphantly.

There is another curious bit of bird lore that I discovered here in the autumn, when, much later than usual, I came back through the lake. Ismaques, when he goes away for the long winter at the South, does not leave

his house to the mercy of the winter storms
until he has first repaired it. Large fresh
sticks are wedged in firmly across the top of
the nest; doubtful ones are pulled out and
carefully replaced, and the whole structure
made shipshape for stormy weather. This
careful repair, together with the fact that the
nest is always well soaked in oil, which preserves it from the rain, saves a deal of trouble
for Ismaques. He builds for life, and knows,
when he goes away in the fall, that, barring
untoward accidents, his house will be waiting
for him with the quiet welcome of old asso-
ciations when he comes back in the spring.
Whether this is a habit of all ospreys, or
only of the two on Big Squatuk Lake — who
were very wise birds in other ways — I am
unable to say.

What becomes of the young birds is also,
to me, a mystery. The home ties are very
strong, and the little ones stay with the
parents much longer than other birds do, as
a rule; but when the spring comes you will
see only the old birds at the home nest. The

83

*Ismaques the
Fishhawk*

young come back to the same general neighborhood, I think; but where the lake is small they never build nor trespass on the same waters. As with the kingfishers, each pair of birds seem to have their own pond or portion; but by what old law of the waters they find and stake their claim is yet to be discovered.

There were two little ones in the nest when I first found it; and I used to watch them in the intervals when nothing was stirring in the underbrush near my hiding place. They were happy, whistling little fellows, well fed and contented with the world. At times they would stand for hours on the edge of the nest, looking down over the slanting tree-tops to the lake, finding the great rustling green world, and the passing birds, and the glinting of light on the sparkling water, and the hazy blue of the distant mountains marvelously interesting, if one could judge from their attitude and their pipings. Then a pair of broad wings would sweep into sight, and they would stretch their wings wide and break into eager whistlings, — *Pip, pip, ch'wee? chip, ch'weeeee?* "did you get him? is he a big one, mother?" And they would stand tiptoeing gingerly about the edge of the great nest, stretching their necks eagerly for a first glimpse of the catch.

85

Ismaques the Fishhawk

At times only one of the old birds would go a-fishing, while the other watched the nest. But when luck was poor both birds would seek the lake. At such times the mother bird, larger and stronger than the male, would fish along the shore, within sight and hearing of her little ones. The male, meanwhile, would go sweeping down the lake to the trout pools at the outlet, where the big chub lived, in search of better fishing grounds. If the wind were strong, you would see a curious bit of sea lore as he came back with his fish. He would never fly straight against the wind, but tack back and forth, as if he had learned the trick from watching the sailor fishermen of the coast beating back into harbor. And, watching him through

---

86

Ismaques the Fishhawk

your glass, you would see that he always carried his fish endwise and head first, so as to present the least possible resistance to the breeze.

While the young were being fed, you were certain to gain new respect for Ismaques by seeing how well he brought up his little ones. If the fish were large, it was torn into shreds and given piecemeal to the young, each of whom waited for his turn with exemplary patience. There was no crowding or pushing for the first and biggest bite, such as you see in a nest of robins. If the fish were small, it was given entire to one of the young, who worried it down as best he could, while the mother bird swept back to the lake for another. The second nestling stood on the edge of the nest meanwhile, whistling good luck and waiting his turn, without a thought, apparently, of seizing a share from his mate beside him.

Just under the hawks a pair of jays had built their nest among the sticks of Ismaques' dwelling, and raised their young on the abundant crumbs which fell from the rich man's table. It was curious and intensely interesting to watch the change which seemed to be going on in the jays' disposition by reason of the unusual friendship. Deedee-askh the jay has not a friend among the wood folk. They all know he is a thief and a meddler, and hunt him away without mercy if they find him near their nests. But the great fishhawks welcomed him, trusted him; and he responded nobly to the unusual confidence. He never tried to steal from the young, not even when the mother bird was away, but contented himself with picking up the stray bits that they had left. And he more than repaid Ismaques by the sharp watch which he kept over the nest, and indeed over all the mountain side. Nothing passes in the woods without the jay's knowledge; and here he seemed, for all the world, like a watchful terrier, knowing that he had only to bark to bring a power of wing and claw sufficient to repel any danger. When prowlers came down from the mountain to

87

Ismaques the Fishhawk

feast on the heads and bones scattered about the foot of the tree, Deedeeaskh dropped down among them and went dodging about, whistling his insatiable curiosity. So long as they took only what was their own, he made no fuss about it; but he was there to watch, and he let them know sharply their mistake, if they showed any desire to cast evil eyes at the nest above.

Once, as my canoe was gliding along the shore, I heard the jays' unmistakable cry of danger. The fishhawks were wheeling in great circles over the lake, watching for the glint of fish near the surface, when the cry came, and they darted away for the nest. Pushing out into the lake, I saw them sweeping above the tree-tops in swift circles, uttering short, sharp cries of anger. Presently they began to swoop fiercely at some animal — a fisher, probably — that was climbing the tree below. I stole up to see what it was; but ere I reached the place they had driven the intruder away. I heard one of the jays far off in the woods, following the robber and

"PRESENTLY THEY BEGAN TO SWOOP
FIERCELY AT SOME ANIMAL"

screaming to let the fishhawks know just
where he was. The other jay sat close by
her own little ones, cowering under the
shadow of the great dark wings above. And
presently Deedeeaskh came back, bubbling
over with the excitement, whistling to them
in his own way that he had followed the ras-
cal clear to his den, and would keep a sharp
watch over him in future.

When a big hawk came near, or when, on
dark afternoons, a young owl took to hunting
in the neighborhood, the jays sounded the
alarm, and the fishhawks swept up from the
lake on the instant. Whether Deedeeaskh
were more concerned for his own young than
for the young fishhawks I have no means of
knowing. The fishermen's actions at such
times showed a curious mixture of fear and
defiance. The mother would sit on the nest
while Ismaques circled over it, both birds
uttering a shrill, whistling challenge. But
they never attacked the feathered robbers,
as they had done with the fisher, and, so far
as I could see, there was no need. Kookoos-

koos the owl and Hawahak the hawk might be very hungry; but the sight of those great wings circling over the nest and the shrill cry of defiance in their ears sent them hurriedly away to other hunting grounds.

There was only one enemy that ever seriously troubled the fishhawks; and he did it in as decent a sort of way as was possible under the circumstances. That was Cheplahgan the eagle. When he was hungry and had found nothing himself, and his two eaglets, far away in their nest on the mountain, needed a bite of fish to vary their diet, he would set his wings to the breeze and mount up till he could see both ospreys at their fishing. There, sailing in slow circles, he would watch for hours till he saw Ismaques catch a big fish, when he would drop like a bolt and hold him up at the point of his talons, like any other highwayman. It was of no use trying to escape. Sometimes Ismaques would attempt it, but the great dark wings would whirl around him and strike down a sharp and unmistakable warning. It always ended the same way. Ismaques, being wise, would drop his fish, and the eagle would swoop down after it, often seizing it ere it reached the water. But he never injured the fishhawks, and he never disturbed the nest. So they got along well enough together. Cheplahgan had a bite of fish now and then in his own way; and honest Ismaques, who never went long hungry, made the best of a bad situation. Which shows that fishing has also taught him patience, and a wise philosophy of living.

93
Ismaques the Fishhawk

The jays took no part in these struggles. Occasionally they cried out a sharp warning as Cheplahgan came plunging down out of the blue, over the head of Ismaques; but they seemed to know perfectly how the unequal contest must end, and they always had a deal of jabber among themselves over it, the meaning of which I could never make out.

As for myself, I am sure that Deedeeaskh could never make up his mind what to think of me. At first, when I came, he would cry out a danger note that brought the fishhawks

94
**Ismaques
the Fishhawk**

circling over their nest, looking down into the underbrush with wild yellow eyes to see what danger threatened. But after I had hidden myself away a few times, and made no motion to disturb either the nest or the hungry prowlers that came to feast on the fishhawks' bounty, Deedeeaskh set me down as an idle, harmless creature who would, nevertheless, bear watching. He never got over his curiosity to know what brought me there. Sometimes, when I thought him far away, I would find him suddenly on a branch just over my head, looking down at me intently. When I went away he would follow me, whistling, to my canoe; but he never called the fishhawks again, unless some unusual action of mine aroused his suspicion; and after one look they would circle away, as if they knew they had nothing to fear. They had seen me fishing so often that they thought they understood me, undoubtedly.

There was one curious habit of these birds that I had never noticed before. Occasionally, when the weather threatened a change, or when the birds and their little ones had fed full, Ismaques would mount up to an enormous altitude, where he would sail about in slow circles, his broad vans steady to the breeze, as if he were an ordinary hen hawk, enjoying himself and contemplating the world from an indifferent distance. Suddenly, with one clear, sharp whistle to announce his intention, he would drop like a plummet for a thousand feet, catch himself in mid-air, and zigzag down to the nest in the spruce top, whirling, diving, tumbling, and crying aloud the while in wild, ecstatic exclamations,—just as a woodcock comes whirling, plunging, twittering down from a height to his brown mate in the alders below. Then Ismaques would mount up again and repeat his dizzy plunge, while his larger mate stood quiet in the spruce top, and the little fishhawks tip-toed about the edge of the nest, *pip-pipping* their wonder and delight at their own papa's dazzling performance.

This is undoubtedly one of Ismaques' springtime habits, by which he tries to win

an admiring look from the keen yellow eyes of his mate; but I noticed him using it more frequently as the little fishhawks' wings spread to a wonderful length, and he was trying, with his mate, by every gentle means to induce them to leave the nest. And I

have wondered — without being able at all to prove my theory — whether he were not trying in this remarkable way to make his little ones want to fly by showing them how wonderful a thing flying could be made to be.

A SCHOOL FOR LITTLE FISHERMEN

A School for Little Fishermen

THERE came a day when, as I sat fishing among the rocks, the cry of the mother osprey changed as she came sweeping up to my fishing grounds, — *Chip, ch'wee! Chip, chip, ch'weeee?* That was the fisherman's hail plainly enough; but there was another note in it, a look-here cry of triumph and satisfaction. Before I could turn my head — for a fish was nibbling — there came other sounds behind it, — *Pip, pip, pip, ch'wee! pip, ch'wee! pip ch'weeee!* — a curious medley, a hail of good-luck cries; and I knew without turning that two other fishermen had come to join the brotherhood.

99

*A School for
Little
Fishermen*

The mother bird — one can tell her instantly by her greater size and darker breast markings — veered in as I turned to greet the newcomers, and came directly over my head, her two little ones flapping lustily behind her. Two days before, when I went down to another lake on an excursion after bigger trout, the young fishhawks were still standing on the nest, turning a deaf ear to all the old birds' assurances that the time had come to use their big wings. The last glimpse I had of them through my glass showed me the mother bird in one tree, the father in another, each holding a fish, which they were showing the young across a tantalizing short stretch of empty air, telling the young, in fishhawk language, to come across and get it; while the young birds, on their part, stretched wings and necks hungrily and tried to whistle the fish over to them, as one would call a dog across the street. In the short interval that I was absent, mother wiles and mother patience had done their good work. The young were already flying

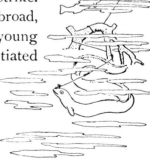
*A School for
Little
Fishermen*

well. Now they were out for their first lesson in fishing, evidently; and I stopped fishing myself, letting my bait sink into the mud — where an eel presently tangled my hooks into an old root — to see how it was done. For fishing is not an instinct with Ismaques, but a simple matter of training. As with young otters, they know only from daily experience that fish, and not grouse and rabbits, are their legitimate food. Left to themselves, especially if one should bring them up on flesh and then turn them loose, they would go straight back to the old hawk habit of hunting the woods, which is much easier. To catch fish, therefore, they must be taught from the first day they leave the nest. And it is a fascinating experience for any man to watch the way they go about it.

The young ospreys flew heavily in short irregular circles, scanning the water with their inexperienced eyes for their first strike. Over them wheeled the mother bird on broad, even wings, whistling directions to the young neophytes, who would presently be initiated

102

*A School for
Little
Fishermen*

into the old sweet mysteries of going a-fishing. Fish were plenty enough; but that means nothing to a fishhawk, who must see his game reasonably near the surface before making his swoop. There was a good jump on the lake, and the sun shone brightly into it. Between the glare and the motion on the surface the young fishermen were having a hard time of it. Their eyes were not yet quick enough to tell them when to swoop. At every gleam of silver in the depths below they would stop short and cry out: *Pip!* "there he is!" *Pip, pip!* "here goes!" like a boy with his first nibble. But a short, clear whistle from the mother stopped them ere they had begun to fall; and they would flap up to her, protesting eagerly that they could catch that fellow, sure, if she would only let them try.

As they wheeled in over me on their way down the lake, one of the youngsters caught the gleam of my pile of chub among the rocks. *Pip, ch'weee!* he whistled, and down they came, both of them, like rockets. They

were hungry; here were fish galore; and
they had not noticed me at all, sitting very
still among the rocks. *Pip, pip, pip, hurrah!*
they piped as they came down.

But the mother bird, who had noted me
and my pile of fish the first thing as she
rounded the point, swept in swiftly
with a curious, half-angry, half-
anxious chiding that I had never heard
from her before,— *Chip chip, chip!
Chip! Chip!*—growing sharper and
shriller at each repetition, till they heeded
it and swerved aside. As I looked up they
were just over my head, looking down at me
now with eager, wondering eyes. Then they
were led aside in a wide circle and talked
to with wise, quiet whistlings before they
were sent back to their fishing again.

And now as they sweep round and round
over the edge of a shoal, one of the little
fellows sees a fish and drops lower to follow
it. The mother sees it too; notes that the
fish is slanting up to the surface, and wisely
lets the young fisherman alone. He is too

near the water now; the glare and the dancing waves bother him; he loses his gleam of silver in the flash of a whitecap. Mother bird mounts higher, and whistles him up where he can see better. But there is the fish again, and the youngster, hungry and heedless, sets his wings for a swoop. *Chip, chip!* "wait, he's going down," cautions the mother; but the little fellow, too hungry to wait, shoots down like an arrow. He is a yard above the surface when a big whitecap jumps up at him and frightens him. He hesitates, swerves, flaps lustily to save himself. Then under the whitecap is a gleam of silver again. Down he goes on the instant, — *ugh! boo!* — like a boy taking his first dive. He is out of sight for a full moment, while two waves race over him, and I hold my breath waiting for him to come up. Then he bursts out, sputtering and shaking himself, and of course without his fish. As he rises heavily the mother, who has been circling over him whistling

advice and comfort, stops short, with a
single blow of her pinions against the air.
She has seen the same fish, watched him
shoot away under the plunge of her little
one, and now sees him glancing up to the
edge of the shoal where the minnows are
playing. She knows that the young pupils
are growing discouraged, and that the time
has come to hearten them. *Chip, chip!* —
"watch, I 'll show you," she whistles —
Cheeeep! with a sharp up-slide at the end,
which I soon grow to recognize as the signal
to strike. At the cry she sets her wings and
shoots downward with strong, even plunge,
strikes a wave squarely as it rises, passes
under it, and is out on the other side, gripping a big chub. The little ones follow her,
whistling their delight, and telling her that
perhaps now they will go back to the nest
and take a look at the fish before they go on
with their fishing. Which means, of course,
that they will eat it and go to sleep perfectly
satisfied with the good fun of fishing; and
then lessons are over for the day.

The mother, however, has other thoughts in her wise head. She knows that the little ones are not yet tired, only hungry; and that there is much to teach them before the chub stop shoaling and they must all be off to the coast. She knows also that they have thus far missed the two things she brought them out to learn: to take a fish always as he comes up; and to hit a wave always on the front side, under the crest. Gripping her fish tightly, she bends in her slow flight and paralyzes it by a single blow in the spine from her hooked beak. Then she drops it back into the whitecaps, where, jumping to the top of my rock, I can see it occasionally struggling near the surface. *Cheeeep!* "try it now," she whistles. *Pip, pip!* "here goes!" cries the little one who failed before; and down he drops, *souse!* going clear under in his impatient hunger, forgetting precept and example and past experience.

Again the waves race over him; but there is a satisfied note in the mother's whistle which tells me that she sees him, and that

"GRIPPING HIS FISH AND *PIP-PIPPING*
HIS EXULTATION"

he is doing well. In a moment he is out again, with a great rush and sputter, gripping his fish and *pip-pipping* his exultation. Away he goes in low heavy flight to the nest. The mother circles over him a moment to be sure he is not overloaded; then she goes back with the other neophyte and ranges back and forth over the shoal's edge.

It is clear now to even my eyes that there is a vast difference in the characters of young fishhawks. The first was eager, headstrong, impatient; the second is calmer, stronger, more obedient. He watches the mother; he heeds her signals. Five minutes later he makes a clean, beautiful swoop and comes up with his fish. The mother whistles her praise as she drops beside him. My eyes follow them as, gossiping like two old cronies, they wing their slow way over the dancing whitecaps and climb the slanting tree-tops to the nest.

The day's lessons are over now, and I go back to my bait catching with a new admiration for these winged members of the

110

A School for Little Fishermen

brotherhood. Perhaps there is also a bit of envy or regret in my meditation as I tie on a new hook to replace the one that an uneasy eel is trying to rid himself of, down in the mud. If I had only had some one to teach me like that, I should certainly now be a better fisherman.

Next day, when the mother came up the lake to the shoal with her two little ones, there was a surprise awaiting them. For half an hour I had been watching from the point to anticipate their coming. There were some things that puzzled me, and that puzzle me still, in Ismaques' fishing. If he caught his fish in his beak, after the methods of mink and otter, I could understand it better. But to catch a fish — whose dart is like lightning — under the water with his feet, when, after his plunge, he can see neither his fish nor his feet, must require some puzzling calculation. And I had set a trap in my head to find out how it is done.

When the fishermen hove into sight, and their eager pipings came faintly up the lake

ahead of them, I paddled hastily out and
turned loose a half-dozen chub in the shallow
water. I had kept them alive as long as
possible in a big pail, and they still had life
enough to fin about near the surface. When
the fishermen arrived I was sitting among the
rocks as usual, and turned to acknowledge
the mother bird's *Ch'wee?* But my deep-
laid scheme to find out their method accom-
plished nothing; except, perhaps, to spoil the
day's lesson. They saw my bait on the instant. One of the youngsters dove headlong
without poising, went under, missed
his fish, rose, plunged again. He got
him that time and went away sputtering. The second took his time,
came down on a long swift slant,
and got his fish without going
under. Almost before the
lesson began it was over.
The mother circled about
for a few moments in a
puzzled sort of way,
watching the young

III

*A School for
Little
Fishermen*

112

*A School for
Little
Fishermen*

fishermen flapping up the slope to their nest. Something was wrong. She had fished enough to know that success means something more than good luck; and this morning success had come too easily. She wheeled slowly over the shallows, noting the fish there, where they plainly did not belong, and dropping to examine with suspicion one big chub that was floating, belly up, on the water. Then she went under with a rush, where I could not see, came out again with a fish for herself, and followed her little ones to the nest.

Next day I set the trap again in the same way. But the mother, with her lesson well laid out before her, remembered yesterday's unearned success and came over to investigate, leaving her young ones circling along the farther shore. There were the fish again, in shallow water; and there — too easy altogether! — were two dead ones floating among the whitecaps. She wheeled away in a sharp turn, as if she had not seen anything, whistled her pupils up to her, and went on to other fishing grounds.

A School for Little Fishermen

Presently, above the next point, I heard their pipings and the sharp, up-sliding *Cheeeep!* which was the mother's signal to swoop. Paddling up under the point in my canoe, I found them all wheeling and diving over a shoal, where I knew the fish were smaller and more nimble, and where there were lily pads for a haven of refuge, whither no hawk could follow them. Twenty times I saw them swoop only to miss, while the mother circled above or beside them, whistling advice and encouragement. And when at last they struck their fish and bore away towards the mountain, there was an exultation in their lusty wing beats, and in the whistling cry they sent back to me, which was not there the day before.

The mother followed them at a distance, veering in when near my shoal to take another look at the fish there. Three were floating now instead of two; the others — what were left of them — struggled feebly at

the surface. *Chip, ch'weee!* she whistled disdainfully; "plenty fish here, but mighty poor fishing." Then she swooped, passed under, came out with a big chub and was gone, leaving me only a blinding splash and a widening circle of laughing, dancing, tantalizing wavelets to tell me how she catches them.

The Partridges' Roll Call

THE PARTRIDGES' ROLL CALL

I WAS fishing, one September afternoon, in the pool at the foot of the lake, trying in twenty ways, as the dark evergreen shadows lengthened across the water, to beguile some wary old trout into taking my flies. They lived there, a score of them, in a dark well among the lily pads, where a cold spring bubbled up from the bottom; and their moods and humors were a perpetual source of worry or amusement, according to the humor of the fisherman himself.

For days at a time they would lie in the deep shade of the lily pads in stupid or sullen indifference. Then nothing tempted them. Flies, worms, crickets, redfins, bumblebees, — all at the end of dainty hair leaders, were drawn with crinkling wavelets over their heads or dropped gently beside them; but

117

118

The Partridges' Roll Call

they only swirled sullenly aside, grouty as King Ahab when he turned his face to the wall and would eat no bread.

At such times scores of little fish swarmed out of the pads and ran riot in the pool. Chub, shiners, "punkin-seeds," perch, boiled up at your flies, or chased each other in savage warfare through the forbidden water, which seemed to intoxicate them by its cool freshness. You had only to swing your canoe up near the shadowy edge of the pool, among the lily pads, and draw your cast once across the open water to know whether or not you would eat trout for breakfast. If the small fish chased your flies, then you might as well go home or study nature; you would certainly get no trout. But you could never tell when the change would come. With the smallest occasion sometimes — a coolness in the air, the run of a cats-paw breeze, a cloud shadow drifting over—a transformation would sweep over the speckled Ahabs lying deep under the lily pads. Some blind, unknown warning would run through the pool before ever a trout had changed his position. Looking over the side of your canoe you would see the little fish darting helter-skelter away among the pads, seeking safety in shallow water, leaving the pool to its tyrant masters. Now is the time to begin casting; your trout are ready to rise.

A playful mood would often follow the testy humor. The plunge of a three-pound fish, the slap-dash of a dozen smaller ones would startle you into nervous casting. But again you might as well spare your efforts, which only served to acquaint the trout with the best frauds in your fly book. They would rush at Hackle or Coachman or Silver Doctor, swirl under it, jump over it, but never take it in. They played with floating leaves; their wonderful eyes caught the shadow of a passing mosquito across the silver mirror of their roof, and their broad tails flung them up to intercept it; but they wanted nothing more than play or exercise, and they would not touch your flies.

120

The Partridges' Roll Call

Once in a way there would come a day when your study and patience found their rich reward. The slish of a line, the flutter of a fly dropping softly on the farther edge of the pool — and then the shriek of your reel, buzzing up the quiet hillside, was answered by a loud snort, as the deer that lived there bounded away in alarm, calling her two fawns to follow. But you scarcely noticed; your head and hands were too full, trying to keep the big trout away from the lily pads, where you would certainly lose him with your light tackle.

On the afternoon of which I write the trout were neither playful nor sullen. No more were they hungry. The first cast of my midget flies across the pool brought no answer. That was good; the little fish had been ordered out, evidently. Larger flies followed; but the big trout neither played with them nor let them alone. They followed cautiously, a foot astern, to the near edge of the lily pads, till they saw me and swirled down again to their cool haunts.

They were suspicious clearly; and with the
lower orders, as with men, the best rule in such a case is to act naturally, with more quietness than usual, and give them time to get over their suspicion.

As I waited, my flies resting among the pads near the canoe, curious sounds came floating down the hillside — *Prut, prut, pr-r-r-rt! Whit-kwit? whit-kwit? Pr-r-rt, pr-r-rt! Ooo-it, ooo-it? Pr-r-reee!* this last with a swift burr of wings. And the curious sounds, half questioning, half muffled in extreme caution, gave a fleeting impression of gliding in and out among the tangled underbrush. "A flock of partridges," I thought, and turned to listen more intently.

The shadows had grown long, with a suggestion of coming night; and other ears than mine had heard the sounds with interest. A swifter shadow fell on the water, and I looked up quickly to see a big owl sail silently out from the opposite hill and perch on a blasted stub overlooking the pool. Kookooskoos had been sleeping in a big

spruce when the sounds waked him, and he started out instantly, not to hunt — it was still too bright — but to locate his game and follow silently to the roosting place, near which he would hide and wait till the twilight fell darkly. I could see it all in his attitude as he poised forward, swinging his round head to and fro, like a dog on an air trail, locating the flock accurately before he should take another flight.

Up on the hillside the eager sounds had stopped for a moment, as if some strange sixth sense had warned the birds to be silent. The owl was puzzled; but I dared not move, because he was looking straight over me. Some faint sound, too faint for my ears, made him turn his head, and on the instant I reached for the tiny rifle lying before me in the canoe. Just as he spread his wings to investigate the new sound, the little rifle spoke, and he tumbled heavily to the shore.

"One robber the less," I was thinking, when the canoe swung slightly on the water. There was a heavy plunge, a vicious rush of my unheeded line, and I seized my rod to find myself fast to a big trout, which had been watching my flies from his hiding among the lily pads till his suspicions were quieted, and the first slight movement brought him up with a rush.

Ten minutes later he lay in my canoe, where I could see him plainly to my heart's content. I was waiting for the pool to grow quiet again, when a new sound came from the underbrush, a rapid *plop, lop, lop, lop, lop,* like the sound in a bottle as water is poured in and the air rushes out.

There was a brook near the sounds, a lazy little stream that had lost itself among the alders and forgotten all its music; and my first thought was that some animal was standing in the water to drink, and waking the voice of the brook as the current rippled past his legs. The canoe glided over to find out what he was, when, in the midst of the sounds, came the unmistakable questioning *Whit-kwit?* of partridges — and there they were, just vanishing glimpses of alert forms

124

*The Partridges'
Roll Call*

and keen eyes gliding among the tangled alder stems. When near the brook they had changed the soft, gossipy chatter, by which a flock holds itself together in the wild tangle of the burned lands, into a curious liquid sound, so like the gurgling of water by a mossy stone that it would have deceived me completely, had I not seen the birds. It was as if they tried to remind the little alder brook of the music it had lost far back among the hills.

Now I had been straitly charged, on leaving camp, to bring back three partridges for our Sunday dinner. My own little flock had grown a bit tired of trout and canned foods; and a taste of young broiled partridges, which I had recently given them, had left them hungry for more. So I left the pool and my fishing rod, just as the trout began to rise, to glide into the alders with my pocket rifle.

There were at least a dozen birds there, full-grown and strong of wing, that had not yet decided to scatter to the four winds, as had most of the coveys which one might meet on the burned lands. All summer long, while berries are plenty, the flocks hold together, finding ten pairs of quiet eyes much better protection against surprises than one frightened pair. Each flock is then under the absolute authority of the mother bird; and one who follows them gets some curious and intensely interesting glimpses of a partridge's education. If the mother bird is killed by owl or hawk or weasel, the flock still holds together, while berries last, under the leadership of one of their own number, more bold or cunning than the others. But with the ripening autumn, when the birds have learned or think they have learned all the sights and sounds and dangers of the wilderness, the covey scatters; partly to cover a wider range in feeding as food grows scarcer; partly in natural revolt at maternal authority, which no bird or animal likes to endure after he has once learned to take care of himself.

125

The Partridges' Roll Call

I followed the flock rapidly, though cautiously, through an interminable tangle of alders that bordered the little stream, and learned some things about them; though they gave me no chance whatever for a rifle shot. The mother was gone; their leader was a foxy bird, the smallest of the lot, who kept them moving in dense cover, running, crouching, hiding, inquisitive about me and watching me, yet keeping themselves beyond reach of harm. All the while the leader talked to them, a curious language of cheepings and whistlings; and they answered back with questions or sharp exclamations as my head appeared in sight for a moment. Where the cover was densest they waited till I was almost upon them before they whisked out of sight; and where there was a bit of opening they whirred up noisily on strong wings, or sailed swiftly away from a fallen log with the noiseless flight that a partridge knows so well how to use when the occasion comes.

Already the instinct to scatter was at work among them. During the day they had

probably been feeding separately along the
great hillside; but with lengthening shadows
they came together again to face the wilderness night in the peace and security of the
old companionship. And I had fortunately
been quiet enough at my fishing to hear
when the leader began to call them together
and they had answered, here and there, from
their feeding.

I gave up following them after a while —
they were too quick for me in the alder
tangle — and came out of the swamp to the
ridge. There I ran along a deer path and
circled down ahead of them to a thicket of
cedar, where
I thought
they might pass the night.

Presently I heard them coming — *Whit-
kwit? pr-r-r, pr-r-r, prut, prut!* — and saw
five or six of them running rapidly. The
little leader saw me at the same instant and
dodged back out of sight. Most of his flock
followed him; but one bird, more inquisitive
than the rest, jumped to a fallen log, drew

himself up straight as a string, and eyed me steadily. The little rifle spoke promptly; and I stowed him away comfortably, a fine plump bird, minus his head, in a big pocket of my hunting shirt.

At the report another partridge, questioning the unknown sound, flew to a thick spruce, pressed close against the trunk to hide himself, and stood listening intently. Whether he was waiting to hear the sound again, or was frightened and listening for the call of the leader, I could not tell. I fired quickly, and saw him sail down against the hillside, with a loud thump and a flutter of feathers behind him to tell me that he was hard hit.

I followed him up the hill, hearing an occasional flutter of wings to guide my feet, till the sounds vanished into a great tangle of underbrush and fallen trees. I searched here ten minutes or more in vain, then listened in the vast silence for a longer period; but the bird had hidden himself away and was watching me, no doubt, out of some covert, where an owl might pass by without finding him. Reluctantly I turned away toward the swamp.

Close beside me was a fallen log; on my right was another; and the two had fallen so as to make the sides of a great angle, their tops resting together against the hill. Between the two were several huge trees growing among the rocks and underbrush. I climbed upon one of these fallen trees and moved along it cautiously, some eight or ten feet above the ground, looking down searchingly for a stray brown feather to guide me to my lost partridge.

Suddenly the log under my feet began to rock gently. I stopped in astonishment, looking for the cause of the strange teetering; but there was nothing on the log beside myself. After a moment I went on again, looking again for my partridge. Again the log rocked, heavily this time, almost throwing me off. Then I noticed that the tip of the other log, which lay balanced across a great rock, was under the tip of my log and was being pried up by something on the other end. Some animal was there, and it flashed upon me suddenly that he was heavy enough to lift my weight with his stout lever. I stole along so as to look behind a great tree — and there on the other log, not twenty feet away, a big bear was standing, twisting himself uneasily, trying to decide whether to go on or go back on his unstable footing.

He discovered me at the instant that my face appeared behind the tree. Such surprise, such wonder I have seldom seen in an animal's face. For a long moment he met my eyes steadily with his. Then he began to twist again, while the logs rocked up and down. Again he looked at the strange animal on the other log; but the face behind the tree had not moved nor changed; the eyes looked steadily into his. With a startled movement he plunged off into the underbrush, and but for a swift grip on a branch the sudden lurch would have sent me off backward among the rocks. As he jumped I heard a swift flutter of wings. I followed it timidly, not knowing where the bear was, and in a moment I had the second partridge stowed away comfortably with his brother in my hunting shirt.

The rest of the flock had scattered widely by this time. I found one or two and followed them; but they dodged away into the thick alders, where I could not find them quick enough with my rifle sight. After a vain, hasty shot or two I went back to my fishing.

Woods and lake were soon quiet again. The trout had stopped rising, in one of their sudden moods. A vast silence brooded over the place, unbroken by any buzz of my noisy reel, and the twilight shadows were growing deeper and longer, when the soft, gliding, questioning chatter of partridges came floating out of the alders. The leader was there, in the thickest tangle — I had learned in an hour to recognize his peculiar *Prut, prut* — and from the hillside and the alder swamp and the big evergreens his flock were answering; here a *kwit*, and there a *prut*, and beyond a swift burr of wings, all drawing closer and closer together.

I had still a third partridge to get for my own hungry flock; so I stole swiftly back into the alder swamp. There I found a little game path and crept along it on hands and knees, drawing cautiously near to the leader's continued calling.

In the midst of a thicket of low black alders, surrounded by a perfect hedge of bushes, I found him at last. He was on the lower end of a fallen log, gliding rapidly up and down, spreading wings and tail and budding ruff, as if he were drumming, and sending out his peculiar call at every pause. Above him, in a long line on the same log, five other partridges were sitting perfectly quiet, save now and then, when an answer came to the leader's call, they would turn their heads and listen intently till the underbrush parted cautiously and another bird flitted up beside them. Then another call,

"THEY WOULD TURN THEIR HEADS
AND LISTEN INTENTLY"

and from the distant hillside a faint *kwit-kwit* and a rush of wings in answer, and another partridge would shoot in on swift pinions to pull himself up on the log beside his fellows. The line would open hospitably to let him in; then the row grew quiet again, as the leader called, turning their heads from side to side for the faint answers.

There were nine on the log at last. The calling grew louder and louder; yet for several minutes now no answer came back. The flock grew uneasy; the leader ran from his log into the brush and back again, calling loudly, while a low chatter, the first break in their strange silence, ran back and forth through the family on the log. There were others to come; but where were they, and why did they tarry? It was growing late; already an owl had hooted, and the roosting place was still far away. *Prut, prut, pr-r-r-ee!* called the leader, and the chatter ceased as the whole flock listened.

I turned my head to the hillside to listen also for the laggards; but there was no

answer. Save for the cry of a low-flying loon and the snap of a twig — too sharp and heavy for little feet to make — the woods were all silent. As I turned to the log again, something warm and heavy rested against my side. Then I knew; and with the knowledge came a swift thrill of regret that made me feel guilty and out of place in the silent woods. The leader was calling, the silent flock were waiting for two of their number who would never answer the call again.

I lay scarcely ten yards from the log on which the sad little drama went on in the twilight shadows, while the great silence grew deep and deeper, as if the wilderness itself were in sympathy and ceased its cries to listen. Once, at the first glimpse of the group, I had raised my rifle and covered the head of the largest bird; but curiosity to know what they were doing held me back. Now a deeper feeling had taken its place; the rifle slid from my hand and lay unnoticed among the fallen leaves.

Again the leader called. The flock drew itself up, like a row of gray-brown statues, every eye bright, every ear listening, till some vague sense of fear and danger drew them together; and they huddled on the ground in a close group, all but the leader, who stood above them, counting them over and over, apparently, and anon sending his cry out into the darkening woods.

I took one of the birds out of my pocket and began to smooth the rumpled brown feathers. How beautiful he was, how perfectly adapted in form and color for the wilderness in which he had lived! And I had taken his life, the only thing he had. Its beauty and something deeper, which is the sad mystery of all life, were gone forever. All summer long he had run about on glad little feet, delighting in nature's abundance, calling brightly to his fellows as they glided in and out in eager search through the lights and shadows. Fear on the one hand, absolute obedience to his mother on the other had been the two great factors of his life.

Between them he grew strong, keen, alert, knowing perfectly when to run and when to fly and when to crouch motionless, as danger passed close with blinded eyes. Then when his strength was perfect, and at last he glided alone through the wilderness coverts in watchful self-dependence — a moment's curiosity, a quick eager glance at the strange animal standing so still under the cedar, a flash, a noise; and all was over. The call of the leader went searching, searching through the woods; but he gave no heed any more.

The hand had grown suddenly very tender as it stroked his feathers. I had taken his life; I must answer for him now. I raised my head and gave the clear *whit-kwit* of a running partridge. Instantly the leader answered; the flock sprang to the log again and turned their heads in my direction to listen. Another call, and now the flock dropped to the ground and lay close, while the leader drew himself up straight on the log and became part of a dead stub beside him.

Something was wrong in my call; the birds were suspicious, knowing not what danger had kept their fellows silent so long, and now threatened them out of the black alders. A moment's intent listening; then the leader stepped slowly down from his log and came towards me cautiously, halting, hiding, listening, gliding, swinging far out to one side and back again in stealthy advance, till he drew himself up abruptly at sight of my face peering out of the underbrush. For a long two minutes he never stirred so much as an eyelid. Then he glided swiftly back, with a faint, puzzled, questioning *kwit-kwit?* to where his flock were waiting. A low signal that I could barely hear, a swift movement — then the flock thundered away in scattered flight into the silent, friendly woods.

Ten minutes later I was crouched in some thick underbrush looking up into a great spruce, when I could just make out the leader standing by an upright branch in sharp silhouette against the glowing west.

I had followed his swift flight, and now lay listening again to his searching call as it went out through the twilight, calling his little flock to the roosting tree. From the swamp and the hillside and far down by the quiet lake they answered, faintly at first, then with clearer call and the whirr of swift wings as they came in.

But already I had seen and heard enough; too much, indeed, for my peace of mind. I crept away through the swamp, the eager calls following me even to my canoe; first a plaint, as if something were lacking to the placid lake and quiet woods and the soft beauty of twilight; and then a faint question, always heard in the *kwit* of a partridge, as if only I could explain why two eager voices would never again answer to roll call when the shadows lengthened.

When You Meet a Bear

When You Meet a Bear

HERE are always two surprises when you meet a bear. You have one, and he has the other. On your tramps and camps in the big woods you may be on the look-out for Mooween; you may be eager and even anxious to meet him; but when you double the point or push into the blueberry patch and, suddenly, there he is, blocking the path ahead, looking intently into your eyes to fathom at a glance your intentions, then, I fancy, the experience is like that of people who have the inquisitive habit of looking under their beds nightly for a burglar, and at last find him there, stowed away snugly, just where they always expected him to be.

*When You Meet
a Bear*

Mooween, on his part, is always looking for you, when once he has learned that you have moved into his woods. But not from any desire to see you! He is like a lazy man looking for work, and hoping devoutly that he may not find it. A bear has very little curiosity — less than any other of the wood folk. He loves to be alone; and so, when he goes hunting for you, to find out just where you are, it is always with the creditable desire to leave you in as large a room as possible, while he himself goes quietly away into deeper solitudes. As this desire of his is much stronger than your mere idle curiosity to see something new, you rarely see Mooween even where he is most at home. And that is but another bit of the poetic justice which you stumble upon everywhere in the big woods.

It is more and more evident, I think, that Nature adapts her gifts, not simply to the necessities, but more largely to the desires, of her creatures. The force and influence of that intense desire — more intense because

usually each animal has but one — we have not yet learned to measure. "Will the unicorn be willing to serve thee, or will he abide by thy crib?" would seem to be the secret of that free life "whose home is the wilderness," if one were quoting Scripture to prove an unprovable theory, as is sometimes our pleasant and unanswerable theological habit. The owl has a silent wing, not simply because he needs it — for his need is no greater than that of the hawk, who has no silent wing — but, more probably, because of his whole-hearted desire for silence as he glides through the silent twilight. And so with the panther's foot; and so with the deer's eye, and the wolf's nose, whose one idea of bliss is a good smell; and so with every other strongly marked gift which the wild things have won from nature, chiefly by wanting it, in the long years of their development.

This theory may possibly account for some of Mooween's peculiarities. Nature, who measures her gifts according to the

145

When You Meet a Bear

146

When You Meet a Bear

desires of her creatures, remembers his love of peace and solitude, and endows him accordingly. He cares little to see you or anybody else; therefore his eyes are weak — his weakest point, in fact. He desires ardently to avoid your society and all society but his own; therefore his nose and ears are marvelously alert to discover your coming. Often, when you think yourself quite alone in the woods, Mooween is there. The wind has told your story to his nose; the clatter of your heedless feet long ago reached his keen ears, and he vanishes at your approach, leaving you to your noise and inquisitiveness and the other things you like. His gifts of concealment are so much greater than your powers of detection that he has absolutely no thought of ever seeing you. His surprise, therefore, when you do meet unexpectedly is correspondingly greater than yours.

What he will do under the unusual circumstances depends largely, not upon himself, but upon you. With one exception, his feelings are probably the reverse of your own. If you are bold, he is timid as a rabbit; if you are panic-stricken, he knows exactly what to do; if you are fearful, he has no fear; if you are inquisitive, he is instantly shy; and, like all other wild creatures, he has an almost uncanny way of understanding your thought. It is as if, in that intent, penetrating gaze of his, he saw your soul turned inside out for his inspection. The only exception is when you meet him without fear or curiosity, with the desire simply to attend to your own affairs, as if he were a stranger and an equal. That rare mental attitude he understands perfectly — for is it not his own? — and he goes his way quietly, as if he had not seen you.

For every chance meeting Mooween seems to have a plan of action ready, which he applies without a question or an instant's hesitation. Make an unknown sound behind him as he plods along the shore, and he hurls himself headlong into the cover of the bushes, as if your voice had touched a button

147

When You Meet a Bear

148

When You Meet a Bear

that released a coiled spring beneath him. Afterwards he may come back to find out what frightened him. Sit perfectly still, and he rises on his hind legs for a look and a long sniff to find out who you are. Jump at him with a yell and a flourish the instant he appears, and he will hurl chips and dirt back at you as he digs his toes into the hillside for a better grip and scrambles away whimpering like a scared puppy.

Once in a way, as you steal through the autumn woods or hurry over the trail, you will hear sudden loud rustlings and shakings on the hardwood ridge above you, as if a small cyclone were perched there for a while, amusing itself among the leaves before blowing on. Then, if you steal up toward the sound, you will find Mooween standing on a big limb of a beech tree, grasping the narrowing trunk with his powerful forearms, tugging and pushing mightily to shake down the ripe beechnuts. The rattle and dash of the falling fruit is such music to

149

When You Meet a Bear

Mooween's ears that he will not hear the rustle of your approach, nor the twig that snaps under your careless foot. If you cry aloud now, under the hilarious impression that you have him sure at last, there is another surprise awaiting you. And that suggests a bit of advice, which is most pertinent: don't stand under the bear when you cry out. If he is a little fellow, he will shoot up the tree, faster than ever a jumping jack went up his stick, and hide in a cluster of leaves, as near the top as he can get. But if he is a big bear, he will tumble down on you before you know what has happened. No slow climbing for him; he just lets go and comes down by gravitation. As Uncle Remus says — who has some keen knowledge of animal ways under his story-telling humor — " Brer B'ar, he scramble 'bout half-way down de bee tree, en den he turn eve'ything loose en hit de groun' *kerbiff!* Look like 't wuz nuff ter jolt de life out'n 'im."

Somehow it never does jolt the life out of him, notwithstanding his great weight; nor

does it interfere in any way with his speed of action, which is like lightning, the instant he touches the ground. Like the coon, who can fall from an incredible distance without hurting himself, Mooween comes down perfectly limp, falling on himself like a great cushion; but the moment he strikes, all his muscles seem to contract at once, and he bounds off like a rubber ball into the densest bit of cover at hand.

Twice have I seen him come down in this way. The first time there were two cubs, nearly full-grown, in a tree. One went up at our shout; the other came down with such startling suddenness that the man who stood ready with his rifle, to shoot the bear, jumped for his life to get out of the way; and before he had blinked the astonishment out of his eyes Mooween was gone, leaving only a violent nodding of the ground spruces to tell what had become of him.

All these plans of ready action in Mooween's head, for the rare occasions when he meets you unexpectedly, are the result of

careful training by his mother. If you
should ever have the good fortune to watch
a mother bear and her cubs when they have
no idea that you are near them, you will note
two characteristic things. First, when they
are traveling — and Mooween is the most
restless tramp in all the woods — you will see
that the cubs follow the mother closely and
imitate her every action with ludicrous exact-
ness, — sniffing where she sniffs, jumping
where she jumps, rising on their hind legs,
with forearms hanging loosely and pointed
noses thrust sharp up into the wind, on the
instant that she rises, and then drawing
silently away from the shore into the shelter
of the friendly alders when some subtle warning tells the mother's nose that the coast
ahead is not perfectly clear. So they learn
to sift the sounds and smells of the wilderness, and to govern their actions accordingly.
And second, when they are playing you will
see that the mother watches the cubs' every
action as keenly as they watched hers an
hour ago. She will sit flat on her

151

When You Meet a Bear

*When You Meet
a Bear*

haunches, her fore paws planted between her outstretched hind legs, her great head on one side, noting every detail of their boxing and wrestling and climbing, as if she had showed them once how it ought to be done and were watching now to see how well they remembered their lessons. And now and then one or the other of the cubs receives a sound cuffing; for which I am unable to account, except on the theory that he was doing something contrary to his plain instructions.

It is only when Mooween meets some new object, or some circumstance entirely outside of his training, that instinct and native wit are set to work; and then you see for the first time some trace of hesitation on the part of this self-confident prowler of the big woods. Once I startled him on the shore, whither he had come to get the fore quarters of a deer that had been left there. He jumped for cover at the first alarm without even turning his head, just as he had seen his mother do a score of times when he was a cub. Then he stopped, and

for three or four seconds considered the danger, in plain sight — a thing I have never seen any other bear imitate. He wavered for a moment more, doubtful whether my canoe were swifter than he and more dangerous. Then satisfied that, at least, he had a good chance, he jumped back, grabbed the deer, and dragged it away into the woods.

Another time I met him on a narrow path where he could not pass me, and where he did not want to turn back, for something ahead was calling him strongly. That short meeting furnished me the best study in bear nature and bear instinct that I have ever been allowed to make. And, at this distance, I have small desire to repeat the experience.

It was on the Little Sou'west Mirimichi, a very wild river, in the heart of the wilderness. Just above my camp, not half a mile away, was a salmon pool that, so far as I know, had never been fished. One bank of the river was an almost sheer cliff, against which the current fretted and hissed in a strong deep rush to the rapids and a great

¹53

When You Meet a Bear

silent pool far below. There were salmon under the cliff, plenty of them, balancing themselves against the arrowy run of the current; but, so far as my flies were concerned, they might as well have been in the Yukon. One could not fish from the opposite shore — there was no room for a back cast, and the current was too deep and swift for wading — and on the shore where the salmon were there was no place to stand. If I had had a couple of good Indians, I might have dropped down to the head of the swift water and fished, while they held the canoe with poles braced on the bottom; but I had no two good Indians, and the one I did have was unwilling to take the risk. So we went hungry, almost within sight and sound of the plunge of heavy fish, fresh run from the sea.

One day, in following a porcupine to see where he was going, I found a narrow path running for a few hundred yards along the side of the cliff, just over where the salmon loved to lie, and not more than thirty feet above the swift rush of water. I went there with my rod and, without attempting to cast, dropped my fly into the current and paid out from my reel. When the line straightened I raised the rod's tip and set my fly dancing and skittering across the surface to an eddy behind a great rock. In a flash I had raised and struck a twenty-five pound fish; and in another flash he had gone straight downstream in the current, where from my precarious seat I could not control him. Down he went, leaping wildly high out of water, in a glorious rush, till all my line buzzed out of the reel, down to the very knot at the bottom, and the leader snapped as if it had been made of spider's web.

I reeled in sadly, debating with myself the unanswerable question of how I should ever have reached down thirty feet to gaff my salmon, had I played him to a standstill. Then, because human nature is weak, I put on a stronger, double leader and dropped another fly into the current. I might not get my salmon; but it was worth the price of

When You Meet a Bear

156

When You Meet a Bear

the leader just to raise him from the deeps and see his terrific rush downstream, jumping, jumping, as if the witch of Endor were astride of his tail in lieu of her broomstick. A lively young grilse plunged headlong at my fly and, thanks to my strong leader, I played him out in the current and led him listlessly, all the jump and fight gone out of him, to the foot of the cliff. There was no apparent way to get down; so, taking my line in hand, I began to lift him bodily up. He came easily enough till his tail cleared the water; then the wiggling, jerky strain was too much. The fly pulled out, and he vanished with a final swirl and slap of his broad tail to tell me how big he was.

Just below me a bowlder lifted its head and shoulders out of the swirling current. With the canoe line I might easily let myself down to that rock and make sure of my next fish. Getting back would be harder; but salmon are worth some trouble; so I left my rod and started back to camp. It was late afternoon, and I was hurrying along the path, giving chief heed to my feet in the ticklish walking, with the cliff above and the river below, when a loud *Hoowuff!* brought me up with a shock. There at a turn in the path, not ten yards ahead, stood a huge bear, calling unmistakable halt, and blocking me in as completely as if the mountain had toppled over before me.

There was no time to think; the shock and scare were too great. I just gasped *Hoowuff!* instinctively, as the bear had shot it out of his deep lungs a moment before, and stood stock-still, as he was doing. He was startled as well as I. That was the only thing that I was sure about.

I suppose that in each of our heads at first there was just one thought: "I'm in a fix; how shall I get out?" And in his training or mine there was absolutely nothing to suggest an immediate answer. He was anxious, evidently, to go on. Something, a mate perhaps, must be calling him up river; else he would have whirled and vanished at the first alarm. But how far might he presume

When You Meet a Bear

on the big animal's timidity, who stood before him blocking the way, and whom he had stopped with his *Hoowuff!* before he should get too near? That was his question, plainly enough. There was no snarl or growl, no savageness in his expression; only intense wonder and questioning in the look which fastened upon my face and seemed to bore its way through, to find out just what I was thinking.

I met his eyes squarely with mine and held them, which was perhaps the most sensible thing I could have done; though it was all unconscious on my part. In the brief moment that followed I did a lot of thinking. There was no escape, up or down; I must go on or turn back. If I jumped forward with a yell, as I had done before under different circumstances, would he not rush at me savagely, as all wild creatures do when cornered? No, the time for that had passed with the first instant of our meeting. The bluff would now be too apparent; it must be done without hesitation, or not at all. If I

turned back, he would follow me to the end
of the ledge, growing bolder as he came
on; and beyond that it was dangerous
walking, where he had all the advantage
and all the knowledge of his ground.
Besides, it was late, and I wanted a salmon
for my supper.

I have wondered since how much of this
hesitation he understood; and how he came
to the conclusion, which he certainly reached,
that I meant him no harm, but only wanted
to get on and was not disposed to give him
the path. All the while I looked at him
steadily, until his eyes began to lose their
intentness. My hand slipped back and
gripped the handle of my hunting knife.
Some slight confidence came with the
motion; though I would certainly have gone
over the cliff and taken my chances in the
current, rather than have closed with him,
with all his enormous strength, in that narrow place. Suddenly his eyes wavered from
mine; he swung his head to look
down and up; and I knew that I

*When You Meet
a Bear*

160

When You Meet a Bear

had won the first move — and the path also, if I could keep my nerve.

I advanced a step or two very quietly, still looking at him steadily. There was a suggestion of white teeth under his wrinkled chops; but he turned his head to look back over the way he had come, and presently he disappeared. It was only for a moment; then his nose and eyes were poked cautiously by the corner of rock. He was peeking to see if I were still there. When the nose vanished again I stole forward to the turn and found him just ahead, looking down the cliff to see if there were any other way below.

He was uneasy now; a low, whining growl came floating up the path. Then I sat down on a rock, squarely in the path, and for the first time some faint suggestion of the humor of the situation gave me a bit of consolation. I began to talk to him, not humorously, but as if he were a Scotchman and open only to argument. "You're in a fix, Mooween, a terrible fix," I kept saying to him softly; "but if you had only stayed at home till twilight, as a bear ought to do, we should be happy now, both of us. You have put me in a fix, too, you see; and now you've just got to get me out of it. I'm not going back. I don't know the path as well as you do. Besides, it will be dark soon, and I should probably break my neck. It's a shame, Mooween, to put any gentleman in such a fix as I am in this minute, just by your blundering carelessness. Why didn't you smell me, anyway, as any but a fool bear would have done, and take some other path over the mountain? Why don't you climb that spruce now and get out of the way?"

I have noticed that all wild animals grow uneasy at the sound of the human voice, speaking however quietly. There is in it something deep, unknown, mysterious beyond all their powers of comprehension; and they go away from it quickly when they can. I have a theory also that all animals, wild and domestic, understand more of our mental attitude than we give them credit for; and

161

When You Meet a Bear

162

When You Meet a Bear

the theory gains rather than loses strength whenever I think of Mooween on that narrow pass. I can see him now, turning, twisting uneasily, and the half-timid look in his eyes as they met mine furtively, as if ashamed; and again the low, troubled whine comes floating up the path and mingles with the rush and murmur of the salmon pool below.

A bear hates to be outdone quite as much as a fox does. If you catch him in a trap, he never growls nor fights nor resists, as lynx and otter and almost all other wild creatures do. He has outwitted you and shown his superiority so often that he is utterly overwhelmed and crushed when you find him, at last, helpless and outdone. He seems to forget all his great strength, all his frightful power of teeth and claws. He just lays his head down between his paws, turns his eyes aside, and refuses to look at you or to let you see how ashamed he is. That is what you are chiefly conscious of, nine times out of ten, when you find a bear

or a fox held fast in your trap; and something of that was certainly in Mooween's look and actions now, as I sat there in his path enjoying his confusion.

Near him a spruce tree sprang out of the rocks and reached upward to a ledge far above. Slowly he raised himself against this, but turned to look at me again sitting quietly in his own path — that he could no longer consider his — and smiling at his discomfiture as I remember how ashamed he is to be outdone. Then an electric shock seemed to hoist him out of the trail. He shot up the tree in a succession of nervous, jerky jumps, rising with astonishing speed for so huge a creature, smashing the little branches, ripping the rough bark with his great claws, sending down a clattering shower of chips and dust behind him, till he reached the level of the ledge above and sprang out upon it; where he stopped and looked down to see what I would do next. And there he stayed, his great head hanging over the edge of the rock, looking at me intently till I rose and went quietly down the trail.

It was morning when I came back to the salmon pool. Unlike the mossy forest floor, the hard rock bore no signs to tell me — what I was most curious to know — whether he came down the tree or found some other way over the mountain. At the point where I had stood when his deep *Hoowuff!* first startled me I left a big salmon, for a taste of which any bear will go far out of his way. Next morning it was gone; and so it may be that Mooween, on his next journey, found another and a pleasanter surprise awaiting him at the turn of the trail.

Quoskh The Keen Eyed

Quoskh the Keen Eyed

SOMETIMES, at night, as you drift along the shore in your canoe, sifting the night sounds and smells of the wilderness, when all harsher cries are hushed and the silence grows tense and musical, like a great stretched chord over which the wind is thrumming low suggestive melodies, a sudden rush and flapping in the grasses beside you breaks noisily into the gamut of half-heard primary tones and rising, vanishing harmonics. Then, as you listen, and before the silence has again stretched the chords of her Eolian harp tight enough for the wind's fingers, another sound, a cry, comes floating down from the air — *Quoskh? quoskh-quoskh?* a wild, questioning call, as if the startled night were asking who

168

Quoskh the Keen Eyed

you are. It is only a blue heron, wakened out of his sleep on the shore by your noisy approach, that you thought was still as the night itself. He circles over your head for a moment, seeing you perfectly, though you catch never a shadow of his broad wings; then he vanishes into the vast, dark silence, crying *Quoskh? quoskh?* as he goes. And the cry, with its strange, wild interrogation vanishing away into the outer darkness, has given him his most fascinating Indian name, Quoskh the Night's Question.

To many, indeed, even to some Indians, he has no other name and no definite presence. He rarely utters the cry by day — his voice then is a harsh croak — and you never see him as he utters it out of the solemn upper darkness; so that there is often a mystery about this voice of the night, which one never thinks of associating with the quiet, patient, long-legged fisherman that one may see any summer day along the borders of lonely lake or stream. A score of times I have been asked by old campers, "What is that?" as a sharp, questioning *Quoskh-quoskh?* seemed to tumble down into the sleeping lake. Yet they knew the great blue heron perfectly — or thought they did.

Quoskh has other names, however, which describe his attributes and doings. Sometimes, when fishing alongshore with my Indian at the paddle, the canoe would push its nose silently around a point, and I would see the heron's heavy slanting flight, already halfway up to the tree-tops, long before our coming had been suspected by the watchful little mother sheldrake, or even by the deer feeding close at hand among the lily pads. Then Simmo, who could never surprise one of the great birds, however silently he paddled, would mutter something which sounded like *Quoskh K'sobeqh*, Quoskh the Keen Eyed. At other times, when we noticed him spearing frogs with his long bill, Simmo, who could not endure the sight of a frog's leg on my fry pan, would speak of him disdainfully in his own musical language as Quoskh the Frog Eater, for my

170

*Quoskh the
Keen Eyed*

especial benefit. Again, if I stopped casting suddenly at the deep trout pool opposite a grassy shore, to follow with my eyes a tall, gray-blue shadow on stilts moving dimly alongshore in seven-league-boot strides for the next bog, where frogs were plenty, Simmo would point with his paddle and say: "See, Ol' Fader Longlegs go catch-um more frogs for his babies. Funny kin' babies dat, eat-um bullfrog; don' chu tink so?"

Of all his names — and there were many more that I picked up from watching him in a summer's outing — "Old Father Longlegs" seemed always the most appropriate. There is a suggestion of hoary antiquity about this solemn wader of our lakes and streams. Indeed, of all birds he is the nearest to those ancient, uncouth monsters which Nature made to people our earth in its uncouth infancy. Other herons and bitterns have grown smaller and more graceful, with shorter legs and necks, to suit our diminishing rivers and our changed landscape. Quoskh is also, undoubtedly, much smaller than he once

was; but still his legs and neck are dispro-
portionately long, when one thinks of the
waters he wades and the nest he builds
and the tracks he leaves in the mud are
startlingly like those fossilized footprints of
giant birds that one finds in the rocks of the
Pliocene era, deep under the earth's surface,
to tell what sort of creatures lived in the
vast solitudes before man came to replenish
the earth and subdue it.

Closely associated with this suggestion of
antiquity in Quoskh's demeanor is the opposite suggestion of perpetual youth which he
carries with him. Age has no apparent effect
on him whatsoever. He is as old and young
as the earth itself is; he is a March day, with
winter and spring in its sunset and sunrise.
Who ever saw a blue heron with his jewel
eye dimmed or his natural force abated? Who
ever caught one sleeping, or saw him totter-
ing weakly on his long legs, as one so often
sees our common wild birds clinging feebly
to a branch with their last grip? A Cape
Cod sailor once told me that, far out from

Quoskh the Keen Eyed

172

land, his schooner had passed a blue heron lying dead on the sea with outstretched wings. That is the only heron that I have ever heard of who was found without all his wits about him. Possibly, if Quoskh ever dies, it may suggest a solution to the question of what becomes of him. With his last strength he may fly boldly out to explore that great ocean mystery, along the borders of which his ancestors for untold centuries lived and moved, back and forth, back and forth, on their endless, unnecessary migrations, restless, unsatisfied, wandering, as if the voice of the sea were calling them whither they dared not follow.

Just behind my tent on the big lake, one summer, a faint, woodsy little trail wandered away into the woods, with endless turnings and twistings, and without the faintest

indication anywhere, till you reached the very
end, whither it intended going. This little
trail was always full of interesting surprises.
Red squirrels peeked down at you over the
edge of a limb, chattering volubly and getting into endless mischief along its borders.
Moose birds flitted silently over it on their
mysterious errands. Now a jumping, smashing, crackling rush through the underbrush
halts you suddenly, with quick beating heart,
as you climb over one of the many windfalls
across your path. A white flag followed by
another little one, flashing, rising, sinking
and rising again over the fallen timber, tells
you that a doe and her fawn were lying
behind the windfall, all unconscious of your
quiet approach. Again, at a turn of the trail,
something dark, gray, massive looms before
you, blocking the faint path; and as you stop
short and shrink behind the nearest tree, a
huge head and antlers swing toward you, with
widespread nostrils and keen, dilating eyes,
and ears like two trumpets pointing straight
at your head — a bull moose, *sh!*

173
*Quoskh the
Keen Eyed*

*Quoskh the
Keen Eyed*

For a long two minutes he stands there motionless, watching the new creature that he has never seen before; and it will be well for you to keep perfectly quiet and let him surrender the path when he is so disposed. Motion on your part may bring him nearer to investigate; and you can never know at what slight provocation the red danger light will blaze into his eyes. At last he moves away, quietly at first, turning often to look and to make trumpets of his ears at you. Then he lays his great antlers back on his shoulders, sticks his nose far up ahead of him, and with long, smooth strides lunges away over the windfalls and is gone.

So every day the little trail had some new surprise for you, — owl, or hare, or prickly porcupine rattling his quills like a quiver of arrows and proclaiming his Indian name, *Unk-wunk! Unk-wunk!* as he loafed along. When you had followed far, and were sure that the loitering trail had certainly lost itself, it crept at last under a dark hemlock; and there, through an oval frame of rustling, whispering green, was the loneliest, loveliest little deer-haunted beaver pond in the world, where Quoskh lived with his mate and his little ones.

The first time I came down the trail and peeked through the oval frame of bushes, I saw him; and the very first glimpse made me jump at the thought of what a wonderful discovery I had made, namely, that little herons play with dolls, as children do. But I was mistaken. Quoskh had been catching frogs and hiding them, one by one, as I came along. He heard me before I knew he was there, and jumped for his last frog, a big fat one, with which he slanted up heavily on broad vans—with a hump on his back and a crook in his neck and his long legs trailing below and behind — towards his nest in the hemlock, beyond the beaver pond. When I saw him plainly he was just crossing the oval frame through which I looked. He had gripped the frog across the middle in his long beak, much as one would hold it with a pair of blunt shears, swelling it out at either

176

Quoskh the Keen Eyed

side, like a string tied tight about a pillow. The head and short arms were forced up at one side, the limp legs dangled down on the other, looking for all the world like a stuffed rag doll that Quoskh was carrying home for his babies to play with.

Undoubtedly they liked the frog much better; but my curious thought about them, in that brief romantic instant, gave me an interest in the little fellows which was not satisfied till I climbed to the nest, long after-. wards, and saw them, and how they lived.

When I took to studying Quoskh, so as to know him more intimately, I found a fascinating subject; not simply because of his queer ways, but also because of his extreme wariness and the difficulties I met in catching him doing things. Quoskh K'sobeqh was the name that at first seemed most appropriate, till I had learned his habits and how best to get the weather of him — which happened only two or three times in the course of a whole summer.

One morning I went early to the beaver pond and sat down against a gray stump on the shore, with berry bushes growing to my shoulders all about me. "Now I shall keep still and see everything that comes," I thought, "and nothing, not even a blue jay, will see me."

That was almost true. Little birds, that had never seen a man in the woods before, came for the berries, and billed them off within six feet of my face before they noticed anything unusual. When they did see me they would turn their heads so as to look at me, first with one eye, then with the other, and shoot up at last, with a sharp *burr!* of their tiny wings, to a branch over my head. There they would watch me keenly, for a wink or a minute, according to their curiosity, then swoop down and whirr their wings loudly in my face, so as to make me move and show what I was.

Across a little arm of the pond, a stone's throw away, a fine buck came to the water, put his muzzle into it, then began to fidget uneasily. Some vague, subtle flavor of me floated across and made him uneasy, though he knew not what I was. He kept tonguing his nostrils, as a cow does, so as to moisten them and catch the scent of me better. On my right, and nearer, a doe was feeding unconcernedly among the lily pads. A mink ran, hopping and halting, along the shore at my feet, dodging in and out among roots and rocks. Cheokhes always runs that way. He knows how glistening black his coat is, how shining a mark he makes for owl and hawk against the sandy shore; and so he never runs more than five feet without dodging out of sight; and he always prefers the roots and rocks that are blackest to travel on.

A kingfisher dropped with his musical *k'plop!* into the shoal of minnows that were rippling the water in their play, just in front of me. Farther out, a fishhawk came down heavily, *souse!* and rose with a big chub. And none of these sharp-eyed wood folk saw me or knew that they were watched. Then a wide, wavy, blue line, like a great Cupid's bow, came gliding swiftly along the opposite bank of green, and Quoskh hove into sight for his morning's fishing.

Opposite me, just where the buck had stood, he folded his great wings; his neck crooked sharply; his long legs, which had been trailed gracefully, straight out behind him in his swift flight, swung under him like two pendulums as he landed lightly on the muddy shore. He knew his ground perfectly; knew every stream and frog-haunted bay in the pond, as one knows his own village; yet no amount of familiarity with his surroundings can ever sing lullaby to Quoskh's watchfulness. The instant he landed he drew himself up straight, standing almost as tall as a man, and let his keen glance run along every shore just once. His head, with its bright yellow eye and long yellow beak glistening in the morning light, veered and swung over his long neck like a gilded weather-vane on a steeple. As the vane swung up the shore toward me I held my

180

Quoskh the Keen Eyed

breath, so as to be perfectly motionless, thinking I was hidden so well that no eye could find me at that distance. As it swung past me slowly I chuckled, thinking that Quoskh was deceived. I forgot altogether that a bird never sees straight ahead. When his bill had moved some thirty degrees off my nose, just enough so as to bring his left eye to bear, it stopped swinging instantly. He had seen me at the first glance, and knew that I did not belong there. For a long moment, while his keen eye seemed to look through and through me, he never moved a muscle. One could easily have passed over him, thinking him only one of the gray, wave-washed roots on the shore. Then he humped himself together, in that indescribably awkward way that all herons have at the beginning of their flight, slanted heavily up to the highest tree on the shore, and stopped for a longer period on a dead branch to look back at me. I had not moved so much as an eyelid; nevertheless he saw me too plainly to trust me. Again he humped himself, rose high over the tree-tops, and bore

away in strong, even, graceful flight for a lonelier lake, where there was no man to watch or bother him.

Quoskh the Keen Eyed

Far from disappointing me, this keenness of Quoskh only whetted my appetite to know more about him, and especially to watch him, close at hand, at his fishing. Near the head of the little bay, where frogs were plenty, I built a screen of boughs under the low thick branches of a spruce tree, and went away to watch other wood folk.

Next morning he did not come back; nor were there any fresh tracks of his on the shore. This was my first intimation that Quoskh knows well the rule of good fishermen, and does not harry a pool or a place too frequently, however good the fishing. The third morning he came back; and again the sixth evening; and then the ninth morning, alternating with great regularity as long as I kept tabs on him. At other times I would stumble upon him, far afield, fishing in other lakes and streams; or see him

Quoskh the Keen Eyed

winging homeward, high over the woods, from waters far beyond my ken; but these appearances were too irregular to count in a theory. I have no doubt, however, that he fished the near-by waters with as great regularity as he fished the beaver pond, and went wider afield only when he wanted a bit of variety, or bigger frogs, as all fishermen do; or when he had poor luck in satisfying the clamorous appetite of his growing brood.

It was on the sixth afternoon that I had the best chance of studying his queer ways of fishing. I was sitting in my little blind at the beaver pond, waiting for a deer, when Quoskh came striding along the shore. He would swing his weather-vane head till he saw a frog ahead, then stalk him slowly, deliberately, with immense caution; as if he knew as well as I how watchful the frogs are at his approach, and how quickly they dive headlong for cover at the first glint of his stilt-like legs. Nearer and nearer he would glide, standing motionless as a gray root when he thought his game was watching

him; then on again more cautiously, bending far forward and drawing his neck back to the angle of greatest speed and power for a blow. A quick start, a thrust like lightning —then you would see him shake his frog savagely, beat it upon the nearest stone or root, glide to a tuft of grass, hide his catch cunningly, and go on unincumbered for the next stalk, his weather-vane swinging, swinging in the ceaseless search for frogs, or possible enemies.

If the swirl of a fish among the sedges caught his keen eye, he would change his tactics, letting his game come to him instead of stalking it, as he did with the frogs. Whatever his position was, both feet down or one foot raised for a stride, when the fish appeared, he never changed it, knowing well that motion would only send his game hurriedly into deeper water. He would stand, sometimes for a half hour, on one leg, letting his head sink slowly down on his shoulders, his neck curled back, his long sharp bill pointing always straight at the quivering

Quoskh the
Keen Eyed

line which marked the playing fish, his eyes half closed till the right moment came. Then you would see his long neck shoot down, hear the splash and, later, the whack of his catch against the nearest root, to kill it; and watch with curious feelings of sympathy as he hid it in the grass and covered it over, lest Hawahak should see, or Cheokhes smell it, and rob him while he fished.

If he were near his last catch, he would stride back and hide the two together; if not, he covered it over in the nearest good place and went on. No danger of his ever forgetting, however numerous the catch! Whether he counts his frogs and fish, or simply remembers the different hiding places, I have no means of knowing.

Sometimes, when I surprised him on a muddy shore and he flew away without taking even one of his tidbits, I would follow his back track and uncover his hiding places to see what he had caught. Frogs, fish, pollywogs, mussels, a baby muskrat, — they were all there, each hidden cunningly under a bit of dried grass and mud. And once I went away and hid on the opposite shore to see if he would come back. After an hour or more he appeared, looking first at my tracks, then at all the shore with greater keenness than usual; then he went straight to three different hiding places that I had found, and two more that I had not seen, and flew away to his nest, a fringe of frogs and fish hanging at either side of his long bill as he went.

He had arranged them on the ground like the spokes of a wheel, as a fox does, heads all out on either side, and one leg or the tail of each crossed in a common pile in the middle; so that he could bite down over the crossed members and carry the greatest number of little frogs and fish with the least likelihood of dropping any in his flight.

The mussels which he found were invariably, I think, eaten as his own particular tidbits; for I never saw him attempt to carry them away, though once I found two or three where he had hidden them. Generally he

Quoskh the Keen Eyed

could crack their shells easily by blows of his powerful beak, or by whacking them against a root; and so he had no need (and probably no knowledge) of the trick, which every gull knows, of mounting up to a height with some obstinate hardshell and dropping it on a rock to crack it.

If Quoskh were fishing for his own dinner, instead of for his hungry nestlings, he adopted different tactics. For them he was a hunter, sly, silent, crafty, stalking his game by approved still-hunting methods; for himself he was the true fisherman, quiet, observant, endlessly patient. He seemed to know that for himself he could afford to take his time and be comfortable, knowing that all things, especially fish, come to him who waits long enough; while for them he must hurry, else their croakings from too long fasting would surely bring hungry, unwelcome prowlers to the big nest in the hemlock.

Once I saw him fishing in a peculiar way, which reminded me instantly of the chumming process with which every mackerel

fisherman on the coast is familiar. He
caught a pollywog for bait, with which he
waded to a deep, cool place under a shady
bank.   There he whacked his pollywog into
small bits and tossed them into the water,
where the chum speedily brought a shoal of
little fish to feed.   Quoskh meanwhile stood
in the shadow, where he would not be noticed,
knee-deep in water, his head drawn down
into his shoulders, and a friendly leafy branch
bending over him to screen him from prying
eyes.   As a fish swam up to his chum he
would spear it like lightning; throw his head
back and wriggle it head-first down his long
neck; then settle down to watch for the next
one.   And there he stayed, alternately watching and feasting, till he had enough; when he
drew his head farther down into his shoulders,
shut his eyes, and went fast asleep in the
cool shadows, — a perfect picture of fishing
indolence and satisfaction.

When I went to the nest and hid myself
in the underbrush to watch day after day,
I learned more of Quoskh's fishing

Quoskh the Keen Eyed

188

Quoskh the Keen Eyed

and hunting. The nest was in a great ever-green, in a gloomy swamp, — a villainous place of bogs and treacherous footing, with here and there a little island of large trees. On one of these islands a small colony of herons were nesting. During the day they trailed far afield, scattering widely, each pair to its own particular fishing grounds; but when the shadows grew long, and night prowlers stirred abroad, the herons came trailing back again, making curious, wavy, graceful lines athwart the sunset glow, to croak and be sociable together, and help each other watch the long night out.

Quoskh the Watchful — I could tell my great bird's mate by sight or hearing from all others, either by her greater size or a pecu-liar double croak she had — had hidden her nest in the top of a great green hemlock. Near by, in the high crotch of a dead tree, was another nest, which she had built, evidently, years before and added to each successive spring, only to abandon it at last for the evergreen. Both birds used to go to the old nest freely; and I have wondered since if it were not a bit of great shrewdness on their part to leave it there in plain sight, where any prowler might see and climb to it; while the young were securely hidden, meanwhile, in the top of the near-by hemlock, where they could see without being seen. Only at a distance could you find the nest. When under the hemlock, the mass of branches screened it perfectly, and your attention was wholly taken by the other nest, standing out in bold relief in the dead tree-top.

Such wisdom, if wisdom it were and not chance, is gained only by experience. It took at least one brood of young herons, sacrificed to the appetite of lucivee or fisher, to teach Quoskh the advantage of that decoy nest to tempt hungry prowlers upon the bare tree bole, where she could have a clear field to spear them with her powerful bill and beat them down with her great wings before they should discover their mistake.

189

Quoskh the Keen Eyed

Quoskh the Keen Eyed

By watching the birds through my glass as they came to the young, I could generally tell what kind of game was afoot for their following. Once a long snake hung from the mother bird's bill; once it was a bird of some kind; twice she brought small animals, whose species I could not make out in the brief moment of alighting on the nest's edge, — all these besides the regular fare of fish and frogs, of which I took no account. And then, one day while I lay in my hiding, I saw the mother heron slide swiftly down from the nest, make a sharp wheel over the lake, and plunge into the fringe of berry bushes on the shore after some animal that her keen eyes had caught moving. There was a swift rustling in the bushes, a blow of her wing to head off a runaway, two or three lightning thrusts of her javelin beak; then she rose heavily, taking a leveret with her; and I saw her pulling it to pieces awkwardly on the nest to feed her hungry little ones.

It was partly to see these little herons, the thought of which had fascinated me ever since I had seen Quoskh taking home what I thought, at first glance, was a rag doll for them to play with, and partly to find out more of Quoskh's hunting habits by seeing what he brought home, that led me at last to undertake the difficult task of climbing the huge tree to the nest. One day, when the mother had brought home some unknown small animal — a mink, I thought — I came suddenly out of my hiding and crossed over to the nest. It had always fascinated me. Under it, at twilight, I had heard the mother heron croaking softly to her little ones — a husky lullaby, but sweet enough to them — and then, as I paddled away, I would see the nest dark against the sunset, with Mother Quoskh standing over it, a tall, graceful silhouette against the glory of twilight, keeping sentinel watch over her little ones. Now I would solve the mystery of the high nest by looking into it.

The mother, alarmed by my sudden appearance, — she had no idea that she had been watched, — shot silently away, hoping I would

Quoskh the Keen Eyed

Quoskh the Keen Eyed

not notice her home through the dense screen of branches. I climbed up with difficulty; but not till I was within ten feet could I make out the mass of sticks above me. The surroundings were getting filthy and evil-smelling by this time; for Quoskh teaches the young herons to keep their nest perfectly clean by throwing all refuse over the sides of the great home. A dozen times I had watched the mother birds of the colony push their little ones to the edge of the nest to teach them this rule of cleanliness, so different from most other birds.

As I hesitated about pushing through the filth-laden branches, something bright on the edge of the nest caught my attention. It was a young heron's eye, looking down at me over a long bill, watching my approach with a keenness that was but thinly disguised by the half-drawn eyelids. I had to go round the tree at this point for a standing on a larger branch; and when I looked up, there was another eye watching down over another long bill. So, however I turned,

they watched me closely getting nearer and
nearer, till I reached up my hand to touch
the nest. Then there was a harsh croak.
Three long necks reached down suddenly
over the edge of the nest on the side where I
was; three long bills opened wide just over my
head; and three young herons grew suddenly
seasick, as if they had swallowed ipecac.

I never saw the inside of that home. At the
moment I was in too much of a hurry to get
down and wash in the lake; and after that, so
large were the young birds, so keen and powerful the beaks, that no man or beast might
expect to look over the edge of the nest, with
hands or paws engaged in holding on, and
keep his eyes for a single instant. It is more
dangerous to climb for young herons than for
young eagles. A heron always strikes for the
eye, and his blow means blindness, or death,
unless you watch like a cat and ward it off.

When I saw the young again they
were taking their
first lessons. A
dismal croaking

194

Quoskh the Keen Eyed

in the tree-tops attracted me and I came over cautiously to see what my herons were doing. The young were standing up on the big nest, stretching necks and wings, and croaking hungrily; while the mother stood on a tree-top some distance away, showing them food and telling them plainly, in heron language, to come and get it. They tried it after much coaxing and croaking; but their long, awkward toes missed their hold upon the slender branch on which she was balancing delicately — just as she expected it to happen. As they fell, flapping lustily, she shot down ahead of them and led them in a long, curving slant to an open spot on the shore. There she fed them with the morsels she held in her beak; brought more food from a tuft of grass where she had hidden it, near at hand; praised them with gurgling croaks till they felt some confidence on their awkward legs; then the whole family started up the shore on their first frogging expedition.

It was intensely interesting for a man who, as a small boy, had often gone a-frogging himself — to catch big ones for a woodsy corn roast, or little ones for pickerel bait — to sit now on a bog and watch the little herons try their luck. Mother Quoskh went ahead cautiously, searching the lily pads; the young trailed behind her awkwardly, lifting their feet like a Shanghai rooster and setting them down with a splash to scare every frog within hearing, exactly where the mother's foot had rested a moment before. So they went on, the mother's head swinging like a weather-vane to look far ahead, the little ones stretching their necks so as to peek by her on either side, full of wonder at the new world, full of hunger for the things that grew there, till a startled young frog said *K'lung!* from behind a lily bud, where they did not see him, and dove headlong into the mud, leaving a long, crinkly, brown trail to tell exactly how far he had gone.

A frog is like an ostrich. When he sees nothing, because his head is hidden, he thinks nothing can see him. At the sudden alarm Mother Quoskh would stretch her neck,

196

Quoskh the Keen Eyed

watching the frog's flight; then turn her head so that her long bill pointed directly at the bump on the smooth muddy bottom, which marked the hiding place of Chigwooltz, and croak softly once. At the sound one of the young herons would hurry forward eagerly; follow his mother's bill, which remained motionless, pointing all the while; twist his head till he saw the frog's back in the mud, and then lunge at it like lightning. Generally he got his frog, and through your glass you would see the unfortunate creature wriggling and kicking his way into Quoskh's yellow beak. If the lunge missed, the mother's keen eye followed the frog's frantic rush through the mud, with a longer trail this time behind him, till he hid again; whereupon she croaked the same youngster up for another try, and then the whole family moved jerkily along, like a row of boys on stilts, to the next clump of lily pads.

As the young grew older, and stronger on their legs, I noticed the rudiments, at least, of a curious habit of dancing, which seems to belong to most of our long-legged wading birds. Sometimes, sitting quietly in my canoe, I would see the young birds sail down in a long slant to the shore. Immediately on alighting, before they gave any thought to frogs or fish or carnal appetite, they would hop up and down, balancing, swaying, spreading their wings, and hopping again round about each other, as if bewitched. A few moments of this crazy performance, and then they would stalk sedately along the shore, as if ashamed of their ungainly levity; but at any moment the ecstasy might seize them and they would hop again, as if they simply could not help it. This occurred generally towards evening, when the birds had fed full and were ready for play or for stretching their broad wings in preparation for the long autumn flight.

Watching them one evening, I remembered suddenly a curious scene that I had stumbled

Quoskh the Keen Eyed

upon when a boy. I had seen a great blue heron sail croaking, croaking, into an arm of the big pond where I was catching bullpouts, and crept down through dense woods to find out what he was croaking about. Instead of one, I found eight or ten of the great birds on an open shore, hopping ecstatically through some kind of a crazy dance. A twig snapped as I crept nearer, and they scattered in instant flight. It was September, and the instinct to flock and to migrate was at work among them. When they came together for the first time some dim old remembrance of generations long gone by — the shreds of an ancient instinct, whose meaning we can only guess at — had set them to dancing wildly; though I doubted at the time whether they understood much what they were doing.

Perhaps I was wrong in this. Watching the young birds at their ungainly hopping, the impulse to dance seemed uncontrollable; yet they were immensely dignified about it at times; and again they appeared to get some fun out of it — as much, perhaps, as

we do out of some of our peculiar dances, of
which a visiting Chinaman once asked inno-
cently: "Why don't you let your servants do
it for you?"

I have seen little green herons do the same
thing in the woods, at mating time; and once,
in the Zoölogical Gardens at Antwerp, I saw
a magnificent hopping performance by some
giant cranes from Africa. Our own sand-hill
and whooping cranes are notorious dancers;
and undoubtedly it is more or less instinctive
with all the tribes of the *Herodiones*, from the
least to the greatest. But what the instinct
means — unless, like our own dancing, it is
a pure bit of pleasure-making, as crows play
games and loons swim races — nobody can
tell.

Before the young were fully grown, and
while yet they were following the mother to
learn the ways of frogging and fishing, a
startling thing occurred, which made me

200

Quoskh the Keen Eyed

ever afterwards look up to Quoskh with honest admiration. I was still-fishing in the middle of the big lake, one late afternoon, when Quoskh and her little ones sailed over the trees from the beaver pond and lit on a grassy shore. A shallow little brook stole into the lake there, and Mother Quoskh left her young to frog for themselves, while she went fishing up the brook under the alders. I was watching the young herons through my glass when I saw a sudden rush in the tall grass near them. All three humped themselves, heron fashion, on the instant. Two got away safely; the other had barely spread his wings when a black animal leaped out of the grass for his neck and pulled him down flapping and croaking desperately.

I pulled up my killick on the instant and paddled over to see what was going on, and what the creature was that had leaped out of the grass. Before my paddle had swung a dozen strokes I saw the alders by the brook open swiftly, and Mother Quoskh sailed out and drove like an arrow straight at the struggling wing tips, which still flapped spasmodically above the grass. Almost before her feet had dropped to a solid landing she struck two fierce, blinding, downward blows of her great wings. Her neck curved back and shot straight out, driving the keen six-inch bill before it, quicker than ever a Roman arm drove its javelin. Above the *lap-lap* of my canoe I heard a savage cry of pain; the same black animal leaped up out of the tangled grass, snapping for the neck; and a desperate battle began, with short gasping croaks and snarls that made caution unnecessary as I sped over to see who the robber was, and how Quoskh was faring in the good fight.

The canoe shot up behind a point, where. looking over the low bank, I had the arena directly under my eye. The animal was a fisher—black-cat the trappers call him—the most savage and powerful fighter of his size in the whole world, I think. In the instant that I first saw him, quicker than thought

Quoskh the
Keen Eyed

he had hurled himself twice, like a catapult, at the towering bird's breast. Each time he was met by a lightning blow in the face from Quoskh's stiffened wing. His teeth ground the big quills into pulp; his claws tore them into shreds; but he got no grip in the feathery mass, and he slipped, clawing and snarling, into the grass, only to spring again like a flash. Again the stiff wing blow; but this time his jump was higher; one claw gripped the shoulder, tore its way through flying feathers to the bone, while his weight dragged the big bird down. Then Quoskh shortened her neck in a great curve. Like a snake it glided over the edge of her own wing for two short, sharp down-thrusts of the deadly javelin — so quick that my eye caught only the double yellow flash of it. With a sharp screech the black-cat leaped away and whirled towards me blindly. One eye was gone; an angry red welt showed just over the other, telling how narrowly the second thrust had missed its mark.—Quoskh's frame seemed to swell, like a hero whose fight is won.

Quoskh the Keen Eyed

A shiver ran over me as I remembered how nearly I had once come myself to the black-cat's condition, and from the same keen weapon. I was a small boy, following a big good-natured hunter that I met in the woods, from pure love of the wilds and for the glory of carrying the game bag. He shot a great blue heron, which fell with a broken wing into soft mud and water grass. Carelessly he sent me to fetch it, not caring to wet his own feet. As I ran up, the heron lay resting quietly, his neck drawn back, his long keen bill pointing always straight at my face. I had never seen so big a bird before, and bent over him, wondering at his long bill, admiring his intensely bright eye.

I did not know then—what I have since learned well—that you can always tell when the rush or spring or blow of any beast or bird—or of any man, for that matter—will surely come, by watching the eye closely. There is a fire that blazes in the eye before the blow comes, before ever a muscle has stirred to do the brain's quick bidding. As I bent over, fascinated by the keen, bright look of the wounded bird, and reached down my hand, there was a flash deep in the eye, like the glint of sunshine from a mirror; and I dodged instinctively. Well for me that I did so. Something shot by my face like lightning, opening up a long red gash across my left temple from eyebrow to ear. As I jumped I heard a careless laugh — "Look out, Sonny, he may bite you — Gosh! what a close call!" And with a white, scared face, as he saw the scar, he dragged me away, as if there had been a bear in the water grass.

The black-cat had not yet received punishment enough. He is one of the largest of the weasel family, and has a double measure of the weasel's savageness and tenacity. He darted about the heron in a quick, nervous, jumping circle, looking for an opening behind; while Quoskh lifted her great torn wings as a shield and turned slowly on the defensive, so as always to face the danger. A dozen

"A DOZEN TIMES THE FISHER JUMPED
FILLING THE AIR WITH FEATHERS"

times the fisher jumped, filling the air with feathers; a dozen times the stiffened wings struck down to intercept his spring, and every blow was followed by a swift javelin thrust. Then, as the fisher crouched snarling in the grass, I saw Mother Quoskh take a sudden step forward, her first offensive move—just as I had seen her twenty times at the finish of a frog stalk—and her bill shot down with the whole power of her long neck behind it. There was a harsh screech of pain; then the fisher wobbled away with blind, uncertain jumps towards the shelter of the woods.

By this time Quoskh had the fight well in hand. A fierce, hot anger seemed to flare within her, as her enemy staggered away, burning out all the previous cool, calculating defense. She started after the fisher, first on the run, then with heavy wing beats, till she headed him and with savage blows of wing and beak drove him back, seeing nothing, guided only by fear and instinct, towards the water. For five minutes more

208

*Quoskh the
Keen Eyed*

she chevied him hither and yon through the trampled grass, driving him from water to bush and back again, jabbing him at every turn; till a rustle of leaves invited him, and he dashed blindly into thick underbrush, where her broad wings could not follow. Then with marvelous watchfulness she saw me standing near in my canoe; and without a thought, apparently, for the young heron lying so still in the grass close beside her, she spread her torn wings and flapped away heavily in the path of her more fortunate younglings.

I followed the fisher's trail into the woods and found him curled up in a hollow stump. He made slight resistance as I pulled him out. All his ferocity was lulled to sleep in the vague, dreamy numbness which Nature always sends to her stricken creatures. He suffered nothing, though he was fearfully wounded; he just wanted to be let alone. Both eyes were gone. There was nothing for me to do, except to finish mercifully what little Quoskh had left undone.

When September came, and family cares were over, the colony beyond the beaver pond scattered widely, returning each one to the shy, wild, solitary life that Quoskh likes best. Almost anywhere, in the loneliest places, I might come upon a solitary heron stalking frogs, or chumming little fish, or treading the soft mud expectantly, like a clam digger, to find where the mussels were hidden by means of his long toes; or just standing still to enjoy the sleepy sunshine till the late afternoon came, when he likes best to go abroad.

210

Quoskh the Keen Eyed

They slept no more on the big nest, standing like sentinels against the twilight glow and the setting moon; but each one picked out a good spot on the shore and slept as best he could on one leg, waiting for the early fishing. It was astonishing how carefully even the young birds picked out a safe position. By day they would stand like statues in the shade of a bank or among the tall grasses, where they were almost invisible by reason of their soft colors, and wait for hours for fish and frogs to come to them. By night each one picked out a spot on the clean open shore, off a point, generally, where he could see up and down, where there was no grass to hide an enemy, and where the bushes were far enough away so that he could hear the slight rustle of leaves before the creature that made it was within springing distance. And there he would sleep safe through the long night, unless disturbed by my canoe or by some other prowler. Herons see almost as well by night as by day; so I could never get near enough to surprise them, however silently I paddled. I would hear only a startled rush of wings, and then a questioning call as they sailed over me before winging away to quieter beaches.

211

Quoskh the Keen Eyed

If I were jacking, with a light blazing brightly before me in my canoe, to see what night folk I might surprise on the shore, Quoskh was the only one for whom my jack had no fascination. Deer and moose, foxes and wild ducks, frogs and fish, — all seemed equally charmed by the great wonder of a light shining silently out of the vast darkness. I saw them all, at different times, and glided almost up to them before timidity drove them away from the strange bright marvel. But Quoskh was not to be watched in that way, nor to be caught by any such trick. I would see a vague form on the far edge of the light's pathway; catch the bright flash of either eye as he swung his weather-vane head; then the vague form would slide into the upper darkness. A moment's waiting; then, above me and behind, where the light did not dazzle

212

Quoskh the Keen Eyed

his eyes, I would hear his night cry—with more of anger than of questioning in it—and as I turned the jack upward I would catch a single glimpse of his broad wings sailing over the lake. Nor would he ever come back, like the fox on the bank, for a second look, to be quite sure what I was.

When the bright moonlit nights came, there was uneasiness in Quoskh's wild breast. The solitary life that he loves best claimed him by day; but at night the old gregarious instinct drew him again to his fellows. Once, when drifting over the beaver pond through the delicate witchery of the moonlight, I heard five or six of the great birds croaking excitedly at the heronry, which they had deserted weeks before. The lake, and especially the lonely little pond at the end of the trail, was lovelier than ever before; but something in the south was calling him away. I think that Quoskh was also moonstruck, as so many wild creatures are; for, instead of sleeping quietly on the shore, he spent his time circling aimlessly over the lake and

woods, crying his name aloud, or calling
wildly to his fellows.

Quoskh the Keen Eyed

At midnight of the day before I broke
camp, I was out on the lake for a last paddle
in the moonlight. The night was perfect,—
clear, cool, intensely still. Not a ripple broke
the great burnished surface of the lake; a
silver pathway stretched away and away over
the bow of my gliding canoe, leading me on
to where the great forest stood, silent, awake,
expectant, and flooded through all its dim,
mysterious arches with marvelous light. The
wilderness never sleeps. If it grow silent, it
is to listen. To-night the woods were tense
as a waiting fox, watching to see what
new thing would come out of the lake, or
what strange mystery would be born under
their own soft shadows.

Quoskh was abroad too, bewitched by the
moonlight. I heard him calling and paddled
down. He knew me long before he was anything more to me than a voice of the night,
and swept up to meet me. For the first time
after darkness fell I saw him — just a vague,

Quoskh the Keen Eyed

gray shadow with edges touched softly with silver light, which whirled once over my canoe and looked down into it. Then he vanished; and from far over on the edge of the waiting woods, where the mystery was deepest, came a cry, a challenge, a riddle, the night's wild question which no man has ever yet answered — *Quoskh? quoskh?*

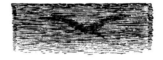

UNK WUNK
THE
PORCUPINE

UNK WUNK THE PORCUPINE

RUSTLING in the brakes just outside my little tent roused me from a light slumber. There it was again! the push of some heavy animal trying to move noiselessly through the tangle close at hand; while from the old lumber camp in the midst of the clearing a low gnawing sound floated up through the still night. I sat up quickly to listen; but at the slight movement all was quiet again. The night prowlers had heard me and were on their guard.

One need have no fear of things that come round in the night. They are much shyer than you are, and can see you better; so

218

Unk
Wunk
The
Porcupine

that, if you blunder towards them, they mistake your blindness for courage, and take to their heels promptly. As I stepped out there was a double rush in some bushes behind my tent, and by the light of a half-moon I caught one glimpse of a bear and her cub jumping away for the shelter of the woods.

The gnawing still went on behind the old shanty by the river. "Another cub!" I thought — for I was new to the big woods — and stole down to peek by the corner of the camp, in whose yard I had pitched my tent, the first night out in the wilderness.

There was an old molasses hogshead lying just beyond, its mouth looking black as ink in the moonlight, and the scratching-gnawing sounds went on steadily within its shadow. "He's inside," I thought with elation, "scraping off the crusted sugar. Now to catch him!"

I stole round the camp, so as to bring the closed end of the hogshead between me and the prize, crept up breathlessly, and with a quick jerk hove the old tub up on end, trapping the creature inside. There was a thump, a startled scratching and rustling, a violent rocking of the hogshead, which I tried to hold down; then all was silent in the trap. "I've got him!" I thought, forgetting all about the old she-bear, and shouted for Simmo to bring the ax.

We drove a ring of stakes close about the hogshead, weighted it down with heavy logs, and turned in to sleep. In the morning, with cooler judgment, we decided that a bear cub was too troublesome a pet to keep in a tent; so I stood by with a rifle while Simmo hove off the logs and cut the stakes, keeping a wary eye on me, meanwhile, to see how far he might trust his life to my nerve. A stake fell; the hogshead toppled over by a push from within; Simmo sprang away with a yell; and out wobbled a big porcupine, the biggest I ever saw, and tumbled away straight towards my tent. After him went the Indian, making sweeping cuts at the stupid thing with his ax, and grunting his derision at my bear cub.

Unk
Wunk
The
Porcupine

Halfway to the tent Unk Wunk stumbled across a bit of pork rind, and stopped to nose it daintily. I caught Simmo's arm and stayed the blow that would have made an end of my catch. Then, between us, Unk Wunk sat up on his haunches, took the pork in his fore paws, and sucked the salt out of it, as if he had never a concern and never an enemy in the wide world. A half hour later he loafed into my tent, where I sat repairing a favorite salmon fly that some hungry sea-trout had torn to tatters, and drove me unceremoniously out of my own bailiwick in his search for more salt.

Such a philosopher, whom no prison can dispossess of his peace of mind, and whom no danger can deprive of his simple pleasures, deserves more consideration than the naturalists have ever given him. I resolved on the spot to study him more carefully. As if to discourage all such attempts and make himself a target for my rifle, he nearly spoiled my canoe the next night by gnawing a hole through the bark and ribs for some suggestion of salt that only his greedy nose could possibly have found.

Unk Wunk
The Porcupine

Once I found him on the trail, some distance from camp, and, having nothing better to do, I attempted to drive him home. My intention was to share hospitality; to give him a bit of bacon, and then study him as I ate my own dinner. He turned at the first suggestion of being driven, came straight at my legs, and by a vicious slap of his tail left some of his quills in me before I could escape. Then I drove him in the opposite direction, whereupon he turned and bolted past me; and when I arrived at camp he was busily engaged in gnawing the end from Simmo's ax handle.

However you take him, Unk Wunk is one of the mysteries. He is a perpetual question scrawled across the forest floor, which nobody pretends to answer; a problem that grows only more puzzling as you study to solve it.

Of all the wild creatures he is the only one that has no fear of man, and that never learns,

222

Unk Wunk The Porcupine

either by instinct or experience, to avoid man's presence. He is everywhere in the wilderness, until he changes what he would call his mind; and then he is nowhere, and you cannot find him. He delights in solitude, and cares not for his own kind; yet now and then you will stumble upon a whole convention of porcupines at the base of some rocky hill, each one loafing around, rattling his quills, grunting his name *Unk Wunk! Unk Wunk!* and doing nothing else all day long.

You meet him to-day, and he is as timid as a rabbit; to-morrow he comes boldly into your tent and drives you out, if you happen to be caught without a club handy. He never has anything definite to do, nor any place to go to; yet stop him at any moment and he will risk his life to go just a foot farther. Now try to drive or lead him another foot in the same direction, and he will bolt back, as full of contrariness as two pigs on a road, and let himself be killed rather than go where he was heading a

moment before. He is perfectly harmless
to every creature ; yet he lies still and kills
the savage fisher that attacks him, or even
the big Canada lynx, that no other creature
in the woods would dare to tackle.

Above all these puzzling contradictions is
the prime question of how Nature ever produced such a creature, and what she intended
doing with him ; for he seems to have no
place nor use in the natural economy of
things. Recently the Maine legislature has
passed a bill forbidding the shooting of porcupines, on the curious ground that he is the
only wild animal that can easily be caught
and killed without a gun; so that a man
lost in the woods need not starve to death.
This is the only suggestion
thus far, from a purely
utilitarian standpoint, that
Unk Wunk is no mistake,
but may have his uses.

Once, to test the law and to provide for
possible future contingencies, I added Unk
Wunk to my bill of fare — a vile, malodorous

Unk Wunk The Porcupine

224

suffix that might delight a lover of strong cheese. It is undoubtedly a good law; but I cannot now imagine any one being grateful for it, unless the stern alternative were death or porcupine.

The prowlers of the woods would eat him gladly enough, but that they are sternly forbidden. They cannot even touch him without suffering the consequences. It would seem as if Nature, when she made this block of stupidity in a world of wits, provided for him tenderly, as she would for a half-witted or idiot child. He is the only wild creature for whom starvation has no terrors. All the forest is his storehouse. Buds and tender shoots delight him in their season; and when the cold becomes bitter in its intensity and the snow packs deep, and all other creatures grow gaunt and savage in their hunger, Unk Wunk has only to climb the nearest tree, chisel off the rough, outer shell with his powerful teeth, and then feed full on the soft inner layer of bark, which satisfies him perfectly and leaves him as fat as an alderman.

Of hungry beasts Unk Wunk has no fear whatever. Generally they let him severely alone, knowing that to touch him would be more foolish than to mouth a sunfish or to bite a peter-grunter. If, driven by hunger in the killing March days, they approach him savagely, he simply rolls up and lies still, protected by an armor that only a steel glove might safely explore, and that has no joint anywhere visible to the keenest eye.

Now and then some cunning lynx or weasel, wise from experience but desperate with hunger, throws himself flat on the ground, close by Unk Wunk, and works his nose cautiously under the terrible bur, searching for the neck or the underside of the body, where there are no quills. One grip of the powerful jaws, one taste of blood in the famished throat — and that is the end of both animals. For Unk Wunk has a weapon that no prowler of the woods ever calculates upon. His broad, heavy tail is armed with hundreds of barbs, smaller but more deadly than those on his back; and he

225
Unk Wunk
The Porcupine

Unk Wunk The Porcupine

swings this weapon with the vicious sweep of a rattlesnake.

Sometimes, when attacked, Unk Wunk covers his face with this weapon. More often he sticks his head under a root or into a hollow log, leaving his tail out ready for action. At the first touch of his enemy the tail snaps right and left quicker than thought, driving head and sides full of the deadly quills, from which there is no escape; for every effort, every rub and writhe of pain, only drives them deeper and deeper, till they rest in heart or brain and finish their work.

Mooween the bear is the only one of the wood folk who has learned the trick of attacking Unk Wunk without injury to himself. If, when very hungry, he finds a porcupine, he never attacks him directly, — he knows too well the deadly sting of the barbs for that, — but bothers and irritates the porcupine by flipping earth at him, until at last he rolls all his quills outward and lies still. Then Mooween, with immense caution, slides one paw under him, and with a quick flip

"BOTHERS AND IRRITATES THE PORCUPINE
BY FLIPPING EARTH AT HIM"

hurls him against the nearest tree, again and again, till all the life is knocked out of him.

If he find Unk Wunk in a tree, he will sometimes climb after him and, standing as near as the upper limbs allow, will push and tug mightily to shake him off. That is usually a vain attempt; for the creature that sleeps sound and secure through a gale in the tree-tops has no concern for the ponderous shakings of a bear. In that case Mooween, if he can get near enough without risking a fall from too delicate branches, will tear off the limb on which Unk Wunk is sleeping and throw it to the ground. That also is usually a vain proceeding; for before he can scramble down after it, Unk Wunk is already up another tree and sleeping, as if nothing had happened, on another branch.

Other prowlers, with less strength and cunning than Mooween, fare badly when driven by famine to attack this useless creature of the woods, for whom Nature nevertheless cares so tenderly. Trappers have told me that in the late winter, when hunger is

Unk Wunk The Porcupine

sharpest, they sometimes catch a wild-cat or lynx or fisher in their traps with his mouth and sides full of porcupine quills, showing to what straits he had been driven for food. These rare trapped animals are but an indication of many a silent struggle that only the trees and stars are witnesses of; and the trapper's deadfall, with its quick, sure blow, is only a merciful ending to what else had been a long, slow, painful trail, ending at last under a hemlock tip with the snow for a covering.

Last summer, in a little glade in the wilderness, I found two skeletons, one of a porcupine, the other of a large lynx, lying side by side. In the latter three quills lay where the throat had been; the shaft of another stood firmly out of an empty eye orbit; a dozen more lay about in such a way that one could not tell by what path they had entered. It needed no great help of imagination to read the story here of a starving lynx, too famished to remember caution, and of a dinner that cost a life.

231
*Unk Wunk
The Porcupine*

Once also I saw a curious bit of animal education in connection with Unk Wunk. Two young owls had begun hunting, under direction of the mother bird, along the foot of a ridge in the early twilight. From my canoe I saw one of the young birds swoop downward at something in the bushes on the shore. An instant later the big mother owl followed with a sharp, angry *hoo-hoo-hoo-hoo!* of warning. The youngster dropped into the bushes; but the mother fairly knocked him away from his game in her fierce rush, and led him away silently into the woods. I went over on the instant, and found a young porcupine in the bushes where the owl had swooped, while two more were eating lily stems farther along the shore.

Evidently Kookooskoos, who swoops by instinct at everything that moves, must be taught by wiser heads the wisdom of letting certain things severely alone.

That he needs this lesson was clearly shown by an owl that my friend once shot at twilight. There was a porcupine quill

Unk Wunk The Porcupine

imbedded for nearly its entire length in his leg. Two more were slowly working their way into his body; and the shaft of another projected from the corner of his mouth. Whether he were a young owl and untaught, or whether, driven by hunger, he had thrown counsel to the winds and swooped at Unk Wunk, will never be known. That he should attack so large an animal as the porcupine would seem to indicate that, like the lynx, hunger had probably driven him beyond all consideration for his mother's teaching.

Unk Wunk, on his part, knows so very little that it may fairly be doubted whether he ever had the discipline of the school of the woods. Whether he rolls himself into a chestnut bur by instinct, as the possum plays dead, or whether that is a matter of slow learning is yet to be discovered. Whether his dense stupidity, which disarms his enemies and brings him safe out of a hundred dangers where wits would fail, is, like the possum's blank idiocy, only a mask for the deepest wisdom; or whether he is quite as stupid as he acts and looks is also a question. More and more I incline to the former possibility. He has learned unconsciously the strength of lying still. A thousand generations of fat and healthy porcupines have taught him the folly of trouble and rush and worry in a world that somebody else has planned, and for which somebody else is plainly responsible. So he makes no effort and lives in profound peace. But this also leaves you with a question, which may take you overseas to explore Hindu philosophy. Indeed, if you have one question when you meet Unk Wunk for the first time, you will have twenty after you have studied him for a season or two. His paragraph in the woods' journal begins and ends with a question mark, and a dash for what is left unsaid.

233

Unk Wunk
The Porcupine

Unk Wunk The Porcupine

The only indication of deliberate plan and effort that I have ever noted in Unk Wunk was in regard to teaching two young ones the simple art of swimming, — which porcupines, by the way, rarely use, and for which there seems to be no necessity. I was drifting along the shore in my canoe when I noticed a mother porcupine and two little ones, a prickly pair indeed, on a log that reached out into the lake. She had brought them there to make her task of weaning them more easy by giving them a taste of lily buds. When they had gathered and eaten all the buds and stems that they could reach, she deliberately pushed both little ones into the water. When they attempted to scramble back she pushed them off again, and dropped in beside them and led them to a log farther down the shore, where there were more lily pads.

The numerous hollow quills floated them high in the water, like so many corks, and they paddled off with less effort than any other young animals that I have ever seen in the water. But whether this were a swimming lesson, or a rude direction to shift and browse for themselves, is still a question. With the exception of one solitary old genius, who had an astonishing way of amusing himself and scaring all the other wood folk, this was the only plain bit of forethought and sweet reasonableness that I have ever found in a porcupine.

235
*Unk Wunk
The Porcupine*

236

A Lazy Fellow's Fun

237

A LAZY FELLOW'S FUN

A NEW sound, a purring rustle of leaves, stopped me instantly as I climbed the beech ridge, one late afternoon, to see what wood folk I might surprise feeding on the rich mast. *Pr-r-r-ush, pr-r-r-ush!* a curious combination of the rustling of squirrels' feet and the soft, crackling purr of an eagle's wings, growing nearer, clearer every instant. I slipped quietly behind the nearest tree to watch and listen.

Something was coming down the hill; but what? It was not an animal running. No

240

A Lazy Fellow's Fun

animal that I knew, unless he had gone suddenly crazy, would ever make such a racket to tell everybody where he was. It was not squirrels playing, nor grouse scratching among the new-fallen leaves. Their alternate rustlings and silences are unmistakable. It was not a bear shaking down the ripe beechnuts — not heavy enough for that, yet too heavy for the feet of any prowler of the woods to make on his stealthy hunting. *Pr-r-r-ush, swish! thump!* Something struck the stem of a bush heavily and brought down a rustling shower of leaves; then out from under the low branches rolled something that I had never seen before, — a heavy grayish ball, as big as a half-bushel basket, so covered over with leaves that one could not tell what was inside. It was as if some one had covered a big kettle with glue and sent it rolling down the hill, picking up dead leaves as it went. So the queer thing tumbled past my feet, purring, crackling, growing bigger and more ragged every moment as it gathered up more leaves, till it reached the bottom of a sharp pitch and lay still.

A Lazy Fellow's Fun

I stole after it cautiously. Suddenly it moved, unrolled itself. Then out of the ragged mass came a big porcupine. He shook himself, stretched, wobbled around a moment, as if his long roll had made him dizzy; then he meandered aimlessly along the foot of the ridge, his quills stuck full of dead leaves, looking big and strange enough to frighten anything that might meet him in the woods.

Here was a new trick, a new problem concerning one of the stupidest of all the wood folk. When you meet a porcupine and bother him, he usually rolls himself into a huge pincushion with all its points outward, covers his face with his thorny tail, and lies still, knowing well that you cannot touch him anywhere without getting the worst of it. Now had he been bothered by some animal and rolled himself up where it was so steep that he lost his balance, and so tumbled unwillingly down the long hill; or, with his

242

A Lazy Fellow's Fun

stomach full of sweet beechnuts, had he rolled down lazily to avoid the trouble of walking; or is Unk Wunk brighter than he looks to discover the joy of roller coasting and the fun of feeling dizzy afterwards?

There was nothing on the hill above, no rustle or suggestion of any hunting animal to answer the question; so I followed Unk Wunk on his aimless wanderings along the foot of the ridge.

A slight movement far ahead caught my eye, and I saw a hare gliding and dodging among the brown ferns. He came slowly in our direction, hopping and halting and wiggling his nose at every bush, till he heard our approach and rose on his hind legs to listen. He gave a great jump as Unk Wunk hove into sight, covered all over with the dead leaves that his barbed quills had picked up on his way downhill, and lay quiet where he thought the ferns would hide him.

The procession drew nearer. Moktaques, full of curiosity, lifted his head cautiously out of the ferns and sat up straight on his haunches again, his paws crossed, his eyes shining in fear and curiosity at the strange animal rustling along and taking the leaves with him. For a moment wonder held him as still as the stump beside him; then he bolted into the bush in a series of high, scared jumps, and I heard him scurrying crazily in a half circle around us.

A Lazy Fellow's Fun

Unk Wunk gave no heed to the interruption, but yew-yawed hither and yon after his stupid nose. Like every other porcupine that I have followed, he seemed to have nothing whatever to do, and nowhere in the wide world to go. He loafed along lazily, too full to eat any of the beechnuts that he nosed daintily out of the leaves. He tried a bit of bark here and there, only to spit it out again. Once he started up the hill; but it was too steep for a lazy fellow with a full stomach. Again he tried it; but it was not steep enough to roll down afterwards. Suddenly he

A Lazy Fellow's Fun

turned and came back to see who it was that followed him about.

I kept very quiet, and he brushed two or three times past my legs, eyeing me sleepily. Then he took to nosing a beechnut from under my foot, as if I were no more interesting than Alexander was to Diogenes.

I had never made friends with a porcupine, — he is too briery a fellow for intimacies, — but now with a small stick I began to search him gently, wondering if, under all that armor of spears and brambles, I might not find a place where it would please him to be scratched. At the first touch he rolled himself together, all his spears sticking straight out on every side, like a huge chestnut bur. One could not touch him anywhere without being pierced by a dozen barbs. Gradually, however, as the stick touched him gently and searched out the itching spots under his armor, he unrolled himself and put his nose under my foot again. He did not want the beechnut; but he did want to nose it out. Unk Wunk is like a pig.

He has very few things to do besides eating; but when he does start to go anywhere or do anything he always does it. Then I bent down to touch him with my hand.

That was a mistake. He felt the difference in the touch instantly. Also he smelled the salt in my hand, for a taste of which Unk Wunk will put aside all his laziness and walk a mile, if need be. He tried to grasp the hand, first with his paws, then with his mouth; but I had too much fear of his great cutting teeth to let him succeed. Instead I touched him behind the ears, feeling my way gingerly through the thick tangle of spines, testing them cautiously to see how easily they would pull out.

The quills were very loosely set in, and every arrow-headed barb was as sharp as a needle. Anything that pressed against them roughly would surely be pierced; the spines would pull out of the skin, and work their way rapidly into the unfortunate hand or paw or nose that touched them. Each spine was like a South Sea Islander's sword, set

A Lazy Fellow's Fun

for half its length with shark's teeth. Once in the flesh it would work its own way, unless pulled out with a firm hand spite of pain and terrible laceration. No wonder Unk Wunk has no fear or anxiety when he rolls himself into a ball, protected at every point by such terrible weapons.

The hand moved very cautiously as it went down his side, within reach of Unk Wunk's one swift weapon. There were thousands of the spines, rough as a saw's edge, crossing each other in every direction, yet with every point outward. Unk Wunk was irritated, probably, because he could not have the salt he wanted. As the hand came within range, his tail snapped back like lightning. I was watching for the blow, but was not half quick enough. At the rustling snap, like the voice of a steel trap, I jerked my hand away. Two of his tail spines came with it; and a dozen more were in my coat sleeve. I jumped away as he turned, and so escaped the quick double swing of his tail

at my legs. Then he rolled into a chestnut
bur again, and proclaimed mockingly at
every point: "Touch me if you dare!"

*A Lazy
Fellow's Fun*

I pulled the two quills with sharp jerks
out of my hand, pushed all the others through
my coat sleeve, and turned to Unk Wunk
again, sucking my wounded hand, which
pained me intensely. "All your own fault,"
I kept telling myself, to keep from whacking him across the nose, his one vulnerable
point, with my stick.

Unk Wunk, on his part, seemed to have
forgotten the incident. He unrolled himself
slowly, and loafed along the foot of the ridge,
his quills spreading and rustling as he went,
as if there were not such a thing as an enemy
or an inquisitive man in all the woods.

He had an idea in his head by this time,
and was looking for something. As I followed close behind him, he would raise himself against a small tree, survey it solemnly
for a moment or two, and go on unsatisfied.
A breeze had come down from the mountain
and was swaying all the tree-tops above him.

248

A Lazy Fellow's Fun

He would look up steadily at the tossing branches, and then hurry on to survey the next little tree he met, with paws raised against the trunk and dull eyes following the motion overhead.

At last he found what he wanted, two tall saplings growing close together and rubbing each other as the wind swayed them. He climbed one of these clumsily, higher and higher, till the slender top bent with his weight towards the other. Then he reached out to grasp the second top with his fore paws, hooked his hind claws firmly into the first, and lay there binding the tree-tops together, while the wind rose and began to rock him in his strange cradle.

Wider and wilder he swung, now stretched out thin, like a rubber string, his quills lying hard and flat against his sides as the tree-tops separated in the wind; now jammed up against himself as they came together again, pressing him into a flat ring with spines sticking straight out, like a

chestnut bur that has been stepped upon.
And there he swayed for a full hour, till it
grew too dark to see him, stretching, contracting, stretching, contracting, as if he were
an accordion and the wind were playing him.
His only note, meanwhile, was an occasional
squealing grunt of satisfaction after some
particularly good stretch, or when the motion
changed and both trees rocked together in
a wide, wild, exhilarating swing.   Now and
then the note was answered, farther down
the ridge, by another porcupine going to
sleep in his lofty cradle.   A storm was coming; and Unk Wunk, who is one of the
wood's best barometers, was crying it aloud
where all might hear.

So my question was answered unexpectedly.   Unk Wunk was out for fun that
afternoon, and had rolled down the hill for
the joy of the swift motion and the dizzy
feeling afterwards, as other wood folk do.
I have watched young foxes, whose den was
on a steep hillside, rolling down one after the
other, and sometimes varying the programme

*A Lazy
Fellow's Fun*

A Lazy Fellow's Fun

by having one cub roll as fast as he could, while another capered alongside, snapping and worrying him in his brain-muddling tumble.

That is all very well for foxes. One expects to find such an idea in wise little heads. But who taught Unk Wunk to roll downhill and stick his spines full of dry leaves to scare the wood folk? And when did he learn to use the tree-tops for his swing and the wind for his motive power?

Perhaps — since most of what the wood folk know is a matter of learning, not of instinct — his mother teaches him some things that we have never yet seen. If so, Unk Wunk has more in his sleepy, stupid head than we have given him credit for, and there is a very interesting lesson awaiting him who shall first find and enter the porcupine school.

UMQUENAWIS
THE MIGHTY

Umquenawis
The Mighty

UMQUENAWIS the Mighty is lord of the woodlands. None other among the wood folk is half so great as he; none has senses so keen to detect a danger, nor powers so terrible to defend himself against it. So he fears nothing, moving through the big woods like a master; and when you see him for the first time in the wilderness pushing his stately, silent way among the giant trees, or plunging like a great engine through under-brush and over windfalls, his nose up to try the wind, his broad antlers far back on his mighty shoulders, while the dead tree that opposes him cracks and crashes down before his rush, and the alders beat a rattling snapping tattoo on his branching horns, — when you see him thus, something within you rises up, like a soldier at salute, and says: "Milord the Moose!" And though the rifle is in your hand, its deadly muzzle never rises from the trail.

That great head with its massive crown is too big for any house. Hung stupidly on a wall, in a room full of bric-a-brac, as you usually see it, with its shriveled ears that were once living trumpets, its bulging eyes that were once so small and keen, and its huge muzzle stretched out of all proportion, it is but misplaced, misshapen ugliness. It has no more, and scarcely any higher, significance than a scalp on the pole of a savage's wigwam. Only in the wilderness, with the irresistible push of his twelve-hundred pound, force-packed body behind it, the crackling underbrush beneath, and the lofty spruce aisles towering overhead, can it give the

"PLUNGING LIKE A GREAT ENGINE THROUGH
UNDERBRUSH AND OVER WINDFALLS"

tingling impression of magnificent power which belongs to Umquenawis the Mighty in his native wilds. There only is his head at home; and only as you see it there, whether looking out in quiet majesty from a lonely point over a silent lake, or leading him in his terrific rush through the startled forest, will your heart ever jump and your nerves tingle in that swift thrill which stirs the sluggish blood to your very finger tips, and sends you quietly back to camp with your soul at peace — well satisfied to leave Umquenawis where he is, rather than pack him home to your admiring friends in a freight car.

Though Umquenawis be lord of the wilderness, there are two things, and two things only, which he sometimes fears: the smell of man, and the spiteful crack of a rifle. For Milord the Moose has been hunted and has learned fear, which formerly he was stranger to. But when you go deep into the wilderness, where no hunter has ever gone, and where the roar of a birch-bark trumpet has never broken the twilight stillness, there you may find him still, as he was before fear came; there he will come smashing down the mountain side at your call, and never circle to wind an enemy; and there, when the mood is on him, he will send you scrambling up the nearest tree for your life, as a squirrel goes when the fox is after him. Once, in such a mood, I saw him charge a little wiry guide, who went up a spruce tree with his snowshoes on — and never a bear did the trick quicker — spite of the four-foot webs in which his feet were tangled.

We were pushing upstream, late one afternoon, to the big lake at the headwaters of a wilderness river. Above the roar of rapids far behind, and the fret of the current near at hand, the rhythmical *clunk, clunk* of the poles and the *lap, lap* of my little canoe as she breasted the ripples were the only sounds that broke the forest stillness. We were silent, as men always are to whom the woods have spoken their deepest message, and to whom the next turn of the river may bring its thrill of unexpected things.

Suddenly, as the bow of our canoe shot round a point, we ran plump upon a big cow moose crossing the river. At Simmo's grunt of surprise she stopped short and whirled to face us. And there she stood, one huge question mark from nose to tail, while the canoe edged in to the lee of a great rock, and hung there quivering, with poles braced firmly on the bottom.

We were already late for camping, and the lake was still far ahead. I gave the word, at last, after a few minutes' silent watching, and the canoe shot upward. But the big moose, instead of making off into the woods, as a well-behaved moose ought to do, splashed straight toward us. Simmo, in the bow, gave a sweeping flourish of his pole, and we all yelled in unison; but the moose came on steadily, quietly, bound to find out what the queer thing was that had just come up river and broken the solemn stillness.

Umquenawis
The Mighty

" Bes' keep still; big moose make-um trouble sometime," muttered Noel behind me; and we dropped back silently into the lee of the friendly rock, to watch awhile longer and let the big creature do as she would.

For ten minutes more we tried every kind of threat and persuasion to get the moose out of the way, ending at last by sending a bullet *zipping* into the water under her body; but beyond an angry stamp of the foot there was no response, and no disposition whatever to give us the stream. Then I bethought me of a trick that I had discovered long before by accident. Dropping down to the nearest bank, I crept up behind the moose, hidden in the underbrush, and began to break twigs, softly at first, then more and more sharply, as if something were coming through the woods fearlessly. At the first suspicious crack the moose whirled, hesitated, started nervously across the stream, twitching her nostrils and wigwagging her big ears to find out what the crackle meant, and hurrying more and more as the sounds grated harshly upon her sensitive nerves. Next moment the river was clear and our canoe was breasting the rippling shallows, while the moose watched us curiously, half hidden in the alders.

Umquenawis The Mighty

261

That is a good trick, for occasions. The animals all fear twig snapping. Only never try it at night, with a bull, in the calling season, as I did once unintentionally. Then he is apt to mistake you for his tantalizing mate, and come down on you like a tempest, giving you a big scare and a monkey scramble into the nearest tree before he is satisfied.

Within the next hour I counted seven moose, old and young, from the canoe; and when we ran ashore at twilight to the camping ground on the big lake, the tracks of an enormous bull were drawn sharply across our landing. The water was still trickling into them, showing that he had just vacated the spot at our approach.

How do I know it was a bull? At this season the bulls travel constantly, and the

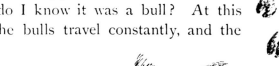

points of the hoofs are worn to a clean, even curve. The cows, which have been living in deep retirement all summer, teaching their ungainly calves the sounds and smells and lessons of the woods, travel much less; and their hoofs, in consequence, are generally long and pointed.

Two miles above our camp was a little brook, with an alder swale on one side and a dark, gloomy spruce tangle on the other — an ideal spot for a moose to keep her little school, I thought, when I discovered the place a few days later. There were tracks on the shore, plenty of them; and I knew I had only to watch long enough to see the mother and her calf, and to catch a glimpse, perhaps, of what no man has ever yet seen clearly; that is, a moose teaching her little one how to hide his bulk; how to move noiselessly and undiscovered through under-brush where, one would think, a fox must make his presence known; how to take a windfall on the run; how to breast down a young birch or maple tree and keep it under

his body while he feeds on the top,—and a
score of other things that every moose must
know before he is fit to take care of himself
in the big woods.

263

*Umquenawis
The Mighty*

I went there one afternoon in my canoe,
grasped a few lily stems to hold the little
craft steady, and snuggled down till only my
head showed above the gunwales, so as to
make canoe and man look as much like an
old, wind-blown log as possible.   It was getting toward the hour when I knew the cow
would be hungry, but while it was yet too
light to bring her little one to the open shore.
After an hour's watching, the cow came cautiously down the brook.   She stopped short
at sight of the big log; watched it steadily
for two or three minutes, wigwagging her
ears; then began to feed greedily on the lily
pads that fringed all the shore.   When
she went back I followed, guided now
by the crack of a twig, now by a swaying of brush tops, now by the flip
of a nervous ear or the push of a
huge dark body, keeping carefully to

leeward all the time, and making the big unconscious creature guide me to where she had hidden her little one.

Just above me, and a hundred yards in from the shore, a tree had fallen, its bushy top bending down two small spruces and making a low den, so dark that an owl could scarcely have seen what was inside. "That's the spot," I told myself instantly; but the mother passed well above it, without noting apparently how good a place it was. Fifty yards farther on she turned and circled back, below the spot, trying the wind with ears and nose as she came on straight towards me.

"Aha! the old moose trick," I thought, remembering how a hunted moose never lies down to rest without first circling back for a long distance, parallel to his trail and to leeward, to find out from a safe distance whether anything is following him. When he lies down, at last, it will be close beside his trail, but hidden from it; so that he hears or smells you as you go by. And when you reach the place, far ahead, where he turned

back he will be miles away, plunging along
down wind at a pace that makes your snow-
shoe swing like a baby's toddle. So you
camp where he lay down, and pick up the
trail in the morning.

265

*Umquenawis
The Mighty*

When the big cow turned and came striding back I knew that I should find her little
one in the spruce den. But would she not
find me, instead, and drive me out of her
bailiwick? You can never be sure what a
moose will do if she finds you near her calf.
Generally they run — always, in fact —
but sometimes they run your way. And
besides, I had been trying for years to see
a mother moose teaching in her little school.
Now I dropped on all fours and crawled away
down wind, so as to get beyond ken of the
mother's inquisitive nose if possible.

She came on steadily, moving with astonishing silence through the tangle, till she
stood where I had been a moment before,
when she started violently and threw her
head up into the wind. Some scent of me
was there, clinging faintly to the leaves and

the moist earth. For a moment she stood like a rock, sifting the air in her nose; then, finding nothing in the wind, she turned slowly in my direction to use her ears and eyes. I was lying very still behind a mossy log by this time, and she did not see me. Suddenly she turned and called, a low bleat. There was an instant stir in the spruce den, an answering bleat, and a moose calf scrambled out and ran straight to the mother. There was an unvoiced command to silence that no human sense could understand. The mother put her great head down to earth — "Smell of that; mark that, and remember," she was saying in her own way; and the calf put his little head down beside hers, and I heard him sniff-sniffing the leaves. Then the mother swung her head savagely, bunted the little fellow out of his tracks, and drove him hurriedly ahead of her away from the place — "Get out, hurry, danger!" was what she was saying now, and emphasizing her teaching with an occasional bunt from behind

that lifted the calf over the hard places.
So they went up the hill, the calf wondering and curious, yet ever reminded by the
hard head at his flank that obedience was
his business just now, the mother turning
occasionally to sniff and listen, till they vanished silently among the dark spruces.

For a week or more I haunted the spot;
but though I saw the pair occasionally, in
the woods or on the shore, I learned no
more of Umquenawis' secrets. The moose
schools are kept in far-away, shady dingles,
beyond reach of inquisitive eyes. Then, one
morning at daylight as my canoe shot round
a grassy point, there were the mother and
her calf standing knee-deep among the lily
pads. With a yell I drove the canoe straight
at the little one.

Now it takes a young moose or caribou a
long time to learn that when sudden danger
threatens he is to follow, not his own frightened head, but his mother's guiding tail.
To young fawns this is practically the first
thing taught by the mothers; but caribou

Umquenawis
The Mighty

are naturally stupid, or trustful, or burningly inquisitive, according to their several dispositions; and moose, with their great strength, are naturally fearless; so that this needful lesson is slowly learned. If you surprise a mother moose or caribou with her young at close quarters, and rush at them instantly, with a whoop or two to scatter their wits, the chances are that the mother will bolt into the brush, where safety lies, and the calf into the lake or along the shore, where the going is easiest.

Several times I have caught young moose and caribou in this way, either swimming or stogged in the mud, and after turning them back to shore have watched the mother's cautious return and her treatment of the lost one. Once I paddled up beside a young bull moose, half grown, and grasping the coarse hair on his back had him tow me a hundred yards, to the next point, while I studied his expression.

'As my canoe shot up to the two moose, they did exactly what I had expected; the mother bolted for the woods in mighty, floundering jumps, mud and water flying merrily about her; while the calf darted along the shore, got caught in the lily pads, and with a despairing bleat settled down in the mud of a soft place, up to his back, and turned his head to see what I was.

269

Umquenawis The Mighty

I ran my canoe ashore and approached the little fellow quietly, without hurry or excitement. Nose, eyes, and ears questioned me; and his fear gradually changed to curiosity as he saw how harmless a thing had frightened him. He even tried to pull his awkward little legs out of the mud in my direction. Meanwhile the big mother moose was thrashing around in the bushes in a terrible swither, calling her calf to come.

I had almost reached the little fellow when the wind brought him the strong scent that he had learned in the woods a few days before, and he bleated sharply. There was an answering crash of brush, a pounding of hoofs that told one unmistakably to look out for his rear, and out of the bushes burst the mother, her eyes red as a wild pig's, and the long hair standing straight up along her back in a terrifying bristle. " Stand not upon the order of your mogging, but mog at once — *eeeunh ! unh !*" she grunted; and I turned otter instantly and took to the lake, diving as soon as the depth allowed and swimming under water to escape the old fury's attention. There was little need of fine tactics, however, as I found out when my head appeared again cautiously. Anything in the way of an unceremonious retreat satisfied her as perfectly as if she had been a Boer general. She went straight to her calf, thrust her great head under his belly, hiked him roughly out of the mud, and then butted him ahead of her into the bushes.

It was stern, rough discipline; but the youngster needed it to teach him the wisdom of the woods. From a distance I

watched the quivering line of brush tops
that marked their course, and then followed
softly. When I found them again, in the
twilight of the great spruces, the mother was
licking the sides of her calf, lest he should
grow cold too suddenly after his unwonted
bath. All the fury and harshness were gone.
Her great head lowered tenderly over the
foolish, ungainly youngster, tonguing him,
caressing him, drying and warming his poor
sides, telling him in mother language that it
was all right now, and that next time he
would do better.

There were other moose on the lake, all
of them as uncertain as the big cow and
her calf. Probably most of them had never
seen a man before our arrival, and it kept
one's expectations on tiptoe to know what
they would do when they saw the strange
two-legged creature for the first time. If a
moose smelled me before I saw him, he
would make off quietly into the woods, as
all wild creatures do, and watch from a
safe distance. But if I stumbled upon him

271

Umquenawis
The Mighty

unexpectedly, when the wind brought no warning to his nostrils, he was fearless, usually, and full of curiosity.

The worst of them all was the big bull whose tracks were on the shore when we arrived. He was a morose, ugly old brute, living apart by himself, with his temper always on edge ready to bully anything that dared to cross his path or question his lordship. Whether he was an outcast, grown surly from living too much alone, or whether he bore some old bullet wound to account for his hostility to man, I could never find out. Far down the river a hunter had been killed, ten years before, by a bull moose that he had wounded; and this may have been, as Noel declared, the same animal, cherishing his resentment with a memory as merciless as an Indian's.

Before we had found this out I stumbled upon the big bull one afternoon, and came near paying the penalty of my ignorance. I had been still-fishing for togue, and was on my way back to camp when, doubling a

point, I ran plump upon a bull moose feeding among the lily pads. My approach had
been perfectly silent, — that is the only way
to see things in the woods, — and he was
quite unconscious that anybody but himself
was near.

He would plunge his great head under
water till only his antler tips showed, and
nose around on the bottom till he found a
lily root. With a heave and a jerk he would
drag it out, and stand chewing it endwise
with huge satisfaction, while the muddy
water trickled down over his face. When
it was all eaten he would grope under the
lily pads for another root in the same way.

Without thinking much of the possible
risk, I began to creep towards him. While
his head was under I would work the
canoe along silently, simply "rolling
the paddle" without lifting it from the
water. At the first lift of his antlers
I would stop and sit low in the canoe
till he finished his juicy morsel and ducked for more.

Then one could slip along easily again without being discovered.

Two or three times this was repeated successfully, and still the big, unconscious brute, facing away from me fortunately, had no idea that he was being watched. His head went under water again — not so deep this time; but I was too absorbed in the pretty game to notice that he had found the end of a root above the mud, and that his ears were out of water. A ripple from the bow of my canoe, or perhaps the faint brush of a lily leaf against the side, reached him. His head burst out of the pads unexpectedly; with a snort and a mighty flounder he whirled upon me; and there he stood quivering, ears, eyes, nose — everything about him reaching out to me and shooting questions at my head with an insistence that demanded instant answer.

I kept quiet, though I was altogether too near the big brute for comfort, till an unfortunate breeze brushed the bow of my canoe still nearer to where he stood, threatening now instead of questioning. The mane on his back began to bristle, and I knew that I had but a small second in which to act. To get speed I swung the bow of the canoe outward, instead of backing away. The movement brought me a trifle nearer, yet gave me a chance to shoot by him. At the first sudden motion he leaped; the red fire blazed out in his eyes, and he plunged straight at the canoe — one, two splashing jumps, and the huge velvet antlers were shaking just over me and the deadly fore foot was raised for a blow.

I rolled over on the instant, startling the brute with a yell as I did so, and upsetting the canoe between us. There was a splintering crack behind me as I struck out for deep water. When I turned, at a safe distance, the bull had driven one sharp hoof through the bottom of the upturned canoe, and was now trying awkwardly to pull his leg out from the clinging cedar ribs. He seemed frightened at the queer, dumb thing that gripped his foot, for he grunted and jumped back, and

275

Umquenawis
The Mighty

thrashed his big antlers in excitement; but he was getting madder every minute.

To save the canoe from being pounded to pieces was now the only pressing business on hand. All other considerations took to the winds in the thought that, if the bull's fury increased and he leaped upon the canoe, as he does when he means to kill, one jump would put the frail thing beyond repair, and we should have to face the dangerous river below in a spruce bark of our own building. I swam quickly to the shore and splashed and shouted and then ran away to attract the bull's attention. He came after me on the instant — *unh! unh! chock, chockety-chock!* till he was close enough for discomfort, when I took to water again. The bull followed, deeper and deeper, till his sides were awash. The bottom was muddy, and he trod gingerly; but there was no fear of his swimming after me. He knows his limits, and they stop him shoulder deep.

When he would follow no farther I swam to the canoe and tugged it out into deep water. Umquenawis stood staring now in astonishment at the sight of this queer man-fish. The red light died out of his eyes for the first time, and his ears wigwagged like flags in the wind. He made no effort to follow, but stood as he was, shoulder deep, staring, wondering, till I landed on the point above, whipped the canoe over, and spilled the water out of it.

277

Umquenawis The Mighty

The paddle was still fast to its cord — as it should always be in trying experiments — and I tossed it into the canoe. The rattle roused Umquenawis from his wonder, as if he had heard the challenging clack of antlers on the alder stems. He floundered out in mighty jumps and came swinging along the shore, *chocking* and grunting fiercely. He had seen the man again, and knew it was no fish — *Unh! unh! eeeeeunh-unh!* he grunted, with a twisting, jerky wriggle of his neck and shoulders at the last squeal, as if he felt me already beneath his hoofs. But before he reached the point

I had stuffed my flannel shirt into the hole in the canoe and was safely afloat once more. He followed along the shore till he heard the sound of voices at camp, when he turned instantly and vanished into the woods.

A few days later I saw the grumpy old brute again in a curious way. I was sweeping the lake with my field glasses when I saw what I thought was a pair of black ducks near a grassy shore. I paddled over, watching them keenly, till a root seemed to rise out of the water between them. Before I could get my glasses adjusted again they had disappeared. I dropped the glasses and paddled faster; they were diving, perhaps — an unusual thing for black ducks — and I might surprise them. There they were again; and there again was the old root bobbing up unexpectedly between them. I whipped my glasses up — the mystery vanished. The two ducks were the tips of Umquenawis' big antlers; the root that rose between them was his head, as he came up to breathe.

It was a close, sultry afternoon; the flies and mosquitoes were out in myriads, and Umquenawis had taken a philosophical way of getting rid of them. He was lying in deep water, over a bed of mud, his body completely submerged. As the swarm of flies that pestered him rose to his head he sunk it slowly, drowning them off. Through my glass, as I drew near, I could see a cloud of them hovering above the wavelets, or covering the exposed antlers. After a few moments there would be a bubbling grumble down in the mud, as Umquenawis blew the air from his great lungs. His head would come up lazily, to breathe among the popping bubbles; the flies would settle upon him like a cloud, and he would disappear again, blinking sleepily as he went down, with an air of immense satisfaction.

It seemed too bad to disturb such comfort, but I wanted to know more about the surly old tyrant that had treated me with such scant courtesy; so I stole near him again,

Umquenawis The Mighty

running up when his head disappeared, and lying quiet whenever he came up to breathe. He saw me at last, and leaped up with a terrible start. There was fear in his eyes this time. Here was the man-fish again, the creature that lived on land or water, and that could approach him so silently that the senses, in which he had always trusted, gave him no warning. He stared hard for a moment; then as the canoe glided rapidly straight towards him without fear or hesitation he waded out, stopping every instant to turn, and look, and try the wind, till he reached the fringe of woods beyond the grasses. There he thrust his nose up ahead of him, laid his big antlers back on his shoulders, and plowed straight through the tangle like a great engine, the alders snapping and crashing merrily about him as he went.

In striking contrast was the next meeting. I was out at midnight, jacking, and passed close by a point where I had often seen the big bull's tracks. He was not there, and I closed the jack and went on along the shore, listening for any wood folk that might be abroad. When I came back a few minutes later, there was a suspicious ripple on the point. I opened the jack, and there was Umquenawis, my big bull, standing out huge and magnificent against the shadowy background, his eyes glowing and flashing in fierce wonder at the sudden brightness. He had passed along the shore within twenty yards of me, through dense underbrush, — as I found out from his tracks next morning, — yet so silently did he push his great bulk through the trees, halting, listening, trying the ground at every step for telltale twigs ere he put his weight down, that I had heard no sound, though I was listening for him intently in the dead hush that was on the lake.

It may have been curiosity, or the uncomfortable sense of being watched and followed by the man-fish, who neither harmed nor feared him, that brought Umquenawis at last to our camp to investigate. One day Noel was washing some clothes of mine in

281

Umquenawis
The Mighty

282

Umquenawis
The Mighty

the lake when some subtle warning made him turn his head. There stood the big bull, half hidden by the dwarf spruces, watching him intently. On the instant Noel left the duds where they were and bolted along the shore under the bushes, calling me loudly to come quick and bring my rifle. When we went back Umquenawis had trodden the clothes into the mud, and vanished as silently as he came.

The Indians grew insistent at this, telling me of the hunter that had been killed, claiming now, beyond a doubt, that this was the same bull, and urging me to kill the ugly brute and rid the woods of a positive danger. But Umquenawis was already learning the fear of me, and I thought the lesson might be driven home before the summer was ended. So it was; but before that time there was almost a tragedy.

One day a timber cruiser — a lonely, silent man with the instincts of an animal for finding his way in the woods, whose business it is to go over timber lands to select the best sites for future cutting — came up to the lake and, not knowing that we were there, pitched by a spring a mile or two below us. I saw the smoke of his camp fire from the lake, where I was fishing, and wondered who had come into the great solitude. That was in the morning. Towards twilight I went down to bid the stranger welcome, and to invite him to share our camp, if he would. I found him stiff and sore by his fire, eating raw-pork sandwiches with the appetite of a wolf. Almost at the same glance I saw the ground about a tree torn up, and the hoof marks of a big bull moose all about. —

"Hello! friend, what's up?" I hailed him.

"Got a rifle?" he demanded, with a rich Irish burr in his voice, paying no heed to my question. When I nodded he bolted for my canoe, grabbed my rifle, and ran away into the woods.

"Queer Dick! unbalanced, perhaps, by living too much alone in the woods," I thought, and took to examining the torn

283

Umquenawis
The Mighty

ground and the bull's tracks to find out for myself what had happened.

But there was no queerness in the frank, kindly face that met mine when the stranger came out of the bush a half hour later. —

"Th' ould baste! he's had me perrched up in that three there, like a blackburrd, the last tin hours; an' divil th' song in me throat or a bite in me stomach. He wint just as you came — I thought I could returrn his compliments wid a bullet," he said, apologetically, as he passed me back the rifle.

Then, sitting by his fire, he told me his story. He had just lit his fire that morning, and was taking off his wet stockings to dry them, when there was a fierce crashing and grunting behind him, and a bull moose charged out of the bushes like a fury. The cruiser jumped and dodged; then, as the bull whirled again, he swung himself into a tree, and sat there astride a limb, while the bull grunted and pushed and hammered the ground below with his sharp hoofs. All day long the moose had kept up the siege, now drawing off cunningly to hide in the bushes, now charging out savagely as the timber cruiser made effort to come down from his uncomfortable perch.

Uniquenawis The Mighty

A few minutes before my approach a curious thing happened; which seems to indicate, as do many other things in the woods, that certain animals — perhaps all animals, including man — have at times an unknown sixth sense, for which there is no name and no explanation. I was still half a mile or more away, hidden by a point and paddling silently straight into the wind. No possible sight or sound or smell of me could have reached any known sense of any animal; yet the big brute began to grow uneasy. He left his stand under the tree and circled nervously around it, looking, listening, wig-wagging his big ears, trying the wind at every step, and setting his hoofs down as if he trod on dynamite. Suddenly he turned and vanished silently into the brush. McGarven, the timber cruiser, who had no idea that there was any man but himself on the lake, watched the bull with growing wonder and distrust, thinking him possessed of some evil demon. In his long life in the woods he had met hundreds of moose, but had never been molested before.

With the rifle at full cock and his heart hot within him, he had followed the trail, which stole away, cautiously at first, then in a long swinging stride straight towards the mountain. — " Oh, 't is the quare baste he is altogether ! " he said as he finished his story.

At the Sound
of the
Trumpet

287

AT THE SOUND OF THE TRUMPET

I T was now near the calling season, and the nights grew keen with excitement. Now and then as I fished, or followed the brooks, or prowled through the woods in the late afternoon, the sudden bellow of a cow moose would break upon the stillness, so strange and uncertain in the thick coverts that I could rarely describe, much less imitate, the sound, or even tell the direction whence it had come. Under the dusk of the lake shore I would

At the Sound of
The Trumpet

sometimes come upon a pair of the huge animals, the cow restless, wary, impatient, the bull now silent as a shadow, now ripping and rasping the torn velvet from his great antlers among the alders, and now threatening and browbeating every living thing that crossed his trail, and even the unoffending bushes, in his testy humor.

One night I went to the landing just below my tent with Simmo and tried for the first time the long call of the cow moose. He and Noel refused absolutely to give it, unless I should agree to shoot the ugly old bull at sight. Several times of late they had seen him near our camp, or had crossed his deep trail on the nearer shores, and they were growing superstitious as well as fearful.

There was no answer to our calling for the space of an hour; silence brooded like a living, watchful thing over sleeping lake and forest, — a

silence that grew only deeper and deeper after the last echoes of the bark trumpet had rolled back on us from the distant mountain. Suddenly Simmo lowered the horn, just as he had raised it to his lips for a call.

At the Sound of The Trumpet

291

"Moose near!" he whispered.

"How do you know?" I breathed; for I had heard nothing.

"Don' know how; just know," he said sullenly. An Indian hates to be questioned, as a wild animal hates to be watched. As if in confirmation of his opinion, there was a startling crash and plunge across the little bay over against us as a bull moose leaped the bank into the lake, within fifty yards of where we crouched on the shore.

"Shoot! shoot-um quick!" cried Simmo; and the fear of the old bull was in his voice. There was a grunt from the moose — a ridiculously small, squeaking grunt, like the voice of a penny trumpet — as the huge creature swung rapidly along the shore in our direction. "Uh! young bull, lil fool moose," whispered Simmo, and breathed

At the Sound of
The Trumpet

a soft, questioning *Whooowuh?* through the bark horn to bring him nearer.

He came close to where we were hidden, then entered the woods and circled silently about our camp to get our wind. In the morning his tracks, within five feet of my rear tent pole, showed how little he cared for the dwelling of man. But though he circled back and forth for an hour, answering Simmo's low call with his ridiculous little grunt, he would not show himself again on the open shore.

I stole up after a while to where I had heard the last twig snap under his hoofs. Simmo held me back, whispering of danger; but there was a question in my head which has never received a satisfactory answer: Why does a bull come to a call anyway? It is held generally — and with truth, I think — that he comes because he thinks the sound is made by a cow moose. But how his keen ears could mistake such a palpable fraud is the greatest mystery in the woods. I have heard a score of hunters and Indians call, all differently, and have sometimes brought a bull into the open at the wail of my own bark trumpet; but I have never yet listened to a call that has any resemblance to the bellow of a cow moose as I have often heard it in the woods. Nor have I ever heard, or ever met anybody who has heard, a cow moose give forth any sound like the "long call" which is made by hunters, and which is used successfully to bring the bull from a distance.

293

At the Sound of The Trumpet

Others claim, and with some reason, that the bull, more fearless and careless at this season than at other times, comes merely to investigate the sound, as he and most other wild creatures do with every queer or unknown thing they hear. The Alaskan Indians stretch a skin into a kind of tambourine and beat it with a club to call a bull; which sound, however, might not be unlike one of the many peculiar bellows that I have heard from cow moose in the wilderness. And I have twice known bulls to come to the *chuck* of an ax on a block; which sound,

294

at a distance, has some resemblance to the peculiar *chock-chocking* that the bulls use to call their mates — just as a turkey cock gobbles, and a partridge drums, and a bull caribou pounds a stump or a hollow tree with the same foolish-fond expectations.

From any point of view the thing has contradictions enough to make one wary of a too positive opinion. Here at hand was a "lil fool moose," who knew no fear, and who might, therefore, enlighten me on the obscure subject. I told Simmo to keep on calling softly, while I crept up into the woods to watch the effect.

It was all as dark as a pocket beyond the open shore. One had to feel his way along, and imitate the moose himself in putting his feet down. Spite of my precaution, a bush swished sharply; a twig cracked. Instantly there was a swift answering rustle ahead as the bull glided towards me.

He had heard the motion and was coming
to see if it were not his tantalizing mate,
ready to whack her soundly, according to his
wont, for causing him so much worry, and to
beat her out ahead of him to the open, where
he could watch her closely and prevent any
more of her hiding tricks.

I stood motionless behind a tree, grasping a branch above, ready to swing up out
of reach when the bull charged. A vague
black hulk thrust itself out of the dark
woods, close in front of me, and stood still.
Against the faint light, which showed from
the lake through the fringe of trees, the
great head and antlers stood out like an
upturned root; but I had never known that
a living creature stood there were it not for
a soft, clucking rumble that the bull kept
going in his throat, — a ponderous kind of
love note, intended, no doubt, to let his
elusive mate know that he was near.

He took another step in my direction,
brushing the leaves softly, a low, whining
grunt telling of his impatience. Two more

295

At the Sound of
The Trumpet

At the Sound of
The Trumpet

steps and he must have discovered me, when fortunately an appealing gurgle and a measured *plop*, *plop*, *plop* — the feet of a moose falling in shallow water — sounded from the shore below, where Simmo was concealed. Instantly the bull turned and glided away, a shadow among the shadows. A few minutes later I heard him running off in the direction whence he had first come.

After that the twilight always found him near our camp. He was convinced that there was a mate hiding somewhere near, and he was bound to find her. We had only to call a few times from our canoe, or from the shore, and presently we would hear him coming, blowing his penny trumpet, and at last see him break out upon the shore with a crashing plunge to waken all the echoes. Then, one night as we lay alongside a great rock in deep shadow, watching the puzzled young bull as he ranged along the shore in the moonlight, Simmo grunted softly to call him nearer. At the sound a larger bull, that we had not suspected, leaped out of the bushes close beside us and splashed straight at the canoe. Only the quickest kind of work saved us. Simmo swung the bow off, with a startled grunt of his own, and I paddled away; while the bull, mistaking us in the dim light for the exasperating cow that had been calling and hiding herself for a week, followed after us into deep water.

There was no doubt whatever that this moose, at least, had come to what he thought was the call of a mate. Moonlight is deceptive beyond a few feet, and when the low grunt sounded in the shadow of the great rock he was sure he had found the coy creature at last, and broke out of his concealment resolved to keep her in sight and not to let her get away again. That is why he swam after us. Had he been investigating

At the Sound of The Trumpet

some new sound or possible danger, he would never have left the land, where alone his great power and his wonderful senses have full play. In the water he is harmless, as most other wild creatures are.

I paddled cautiously just ahead of him, so near that, looking over my shoulder, I could see the flash of his eye and the waves crinkling away before the push of his great nose. After a short swim he grew suspicious of the queer thing that kept just so far ahead, whether he swam fast or slow, and turned in towards the shore, whining his impatience. I followed slowly, letting him get some distance ahead, and just as his feet struck bottom whispered to Simmo for his most seductive gurgle. At the call the bull whirled and plunged after us again recklessly, and I led him across to where the younger bull was still ranging up and down the shore, calling imploringly to his phantom mate.

I expected a battle when the two rivals should meet; but they paid little attention to each other. The common misfortune, or the common misery, seemed to kill the fierce natural jealousy whose fury I had more than once been witness of. They had lost all fear by this time; they ranged up and down the shore, or smashed recklessly through the swamps, as the elusive smells and echoes called them hither and yon in their frantic search.

Far up on the mountain side the sharp, challenging grunt of a master bull broke out of the startled woods in one of the lulls of our exciting play. Simmo heard, and turned in the bow to whisper excitedly: " Nother bull! Fetch-um Ol' Dev'l this time, sartin." Raising his horn, he gave the long, rolling bellow of a cow moose. A fiercer trumpet call from the mountain side answered; then the sound was lost in the *crash-crash* of the first two bulls, as they broke out upon the shore on opposite sides of the canoe.

We gave little heed now to the nearer play; our whole

299

At the Sound of The Trumpet

attention was fixed on a hoarse, grunting roar
— *Uh, uh, uh! erryuh! r-r-r-runh-unh!* —
with a rattling, snapping crash of underbrush
for an accompaniment. The younger bull
heard it; listened for a moment, like a great
black statue under the moonlight; then he
glided away into the shadows under the bank.
The larger bull heard it and came swinging
along the shore, hurling a savage challenge
back on the echoing woods at every stride.

There was an ominous silence up on the
ridge where a moment before all was fierce
commotion. Simmo was silent too; the
uproar had been appalling, with the sleeping
lake below us, and the vast forest, where
silence dwells at home, stretching up and
away on every hand to the sky line. But
the spirit of mischief was tingling all over
me as I seized the horn and gave the low
appealing grunt that a cow would have
uttered under the same circumstances. Like
a shot the answer was hurled back, and
down came the great bull — smash, crack,
r-r-runh! till he burst like a tempest out

"A MIGHTY SPRING OF HIS CROUCHING
HAUNCHES FINISHED THE WORK"

on the open shore, where the second bull with a challenging roar leaped to meet him.

Simmo was begging me to shoot, shoot, telling me excitedly that "Ol' Dev'l," as he called him, would be more dangerous now than ever, if I let him get away; but I only drove the canoe in closer to the splashing, grunting uproar among the shadows under the bank.

There was a terrific duel under way when I swung the canoe alongside a moment later. The bulls crashed together with a shock to break their heads. Mud and water flew over them; their great antlers clashed and rang like metal blades as they pushed and tugged, grunting like demons in the fierce struggle. But the contest was too one-sided to last long. Ol' Dev'l had smashed down from the mountain in a frightful rage, and with a power that nothing could resist. With a quick lunge he locked antlers in the grip he wanted; a twist of his massive neck and shoulders forced the opposing head aside, and a mighty spring of his crouching

At the Sound of
The Trumpet

haunches finished the work. The second moose went over with a plunge like a bolt-struck pine. As he rolled up to his feet again the savage old bull jumped for him, and drove the brow antlers into his flanks. The next moment both bulls had crashed away into the woods, one swinging off in giant strides through the crackling under-brush for his life, the other close behind, charging like a battering-ram into his enemy's rear, grunting like a huge wild boar in his rage and exultation. So the chase vanished over the ridge into the valley beyond; and silence stole back, like a Chinese empress, into her disturbed dominions.

From behind a great windfall on the point above, the first young bull stole out, and came halting and listening along the shore to the scene of the conflict. " To the discreet belong the spoils " was written in every timorous step and stealthy movement. A low grunt from my horn reassured him; he grew confident; now he would find the phantom mate that had occasioned so much trouble, and run away with her before the conqueror should return from his chase. He swung along rapidly, rumbling the low call in his throat. Then up on the ridge sounded again the crackle of brush and the roar of a challenge. Ol' Dev'l was coming back for his reward. On the instant all confidence vanished from the young bull's attitude. He slipped away into the woods. There was no sound; scarcely a definite motion. A shadow seemed to glide away into the darker shadows. The underbrush closed softly behind it, and he was gone.

Next morning at daybreak I found my old bull on the shore, a mile below; and with him was the great cow that had hunted me away from her little one, which still followed her about obediently. I left them there undisturbed, with a thought of the mighty offspring that shall some day come smashing down from the mountain to delight

305

At the Sound of The Trumpet

the heart of camper or hunter and set his nerves a-tingle, when the lake shall again be visited, and the roar of a bark trumpet roll over the sleeping lake and the startled woods. Let them kill who will. I have seen Umquenawis the Mighty as he was before fear came, and am satisfied.

THE GLADSOME LIFE

307

The Gladsome Life

OVER my head soared an eagle one day, his broad vans set firm to the breeze that was doing his pleasure splendidly, keeping him afloat in the blue, just where he wanted to be. At my feet sprawled a turtle, enjoying himself in his own way. The two together taught me a lesson, which I am glad now to remember.

The morning fishing was over. A couple of grilse, beautiful four-pound fish, fresh from the sea, lay snug together in my fish basket — enough for the day and to spare.

310

The Gladsome Life

So I gave up — with an effort, I must confess — the big salmon that had plunged twice at my Jock Scott, and sat down on a stranded log to enjoy myself, as the wood folk were doing all about me.

The river rippled past with strong, even sweep. Below was the deep pool, with smiles and glintings of light on its dark face, where the salmon, after their long run from the sea, rested awhile before taking up their positions in the swift water, in which they love to lie, balancing themselves against the rush and tremor of the current. Above were the riffles, making white foam patches of the water, as if they were having a soap-bubble party all to themselves. The big white bubbles would come dancing, swinging down to the eddies behind the rocks, where a playful young grilse would shoot up through them, scattering them merrily, and adding a dozen more bubbles and wimples to the running troop as he fell back into his eddy with a musical splash that set all the warblers on the bank to whistling. Now and then a big white patch would escape all this and enter sedately the swift run of water along the great ledge on the farther shore. My big salmon lived there; and just as the foam patch dipped sharply into the quiet water below, he would swirl under it and knock it into smithereens with a blow of his tail.

So the play went on, while I sat watching it — watching the shadows, watching the dabs and pencilings of light and the changing reflections, watching the foam bubbles with special delight and anticipation, betting with myself how far they would run, whether to the second eddy or to the rim of the pool, before the salmon would smash them in their play. Then a shadow fell on the water, and I looked up to watch the great eagle breasting, balancing, playing with the mighty air currents above, as the fishes played in the swift rush of water below.

He set his wings square to the wind at first and slanted swiftly up, like a well hung

312

The
Gladsome
Life

kite. But that was too fast for leisure hours. He had only dropped down to the pool in idle curiosity to see what was doing. Then, watching his wing tips keenly through my glass, I saw the quills turn ever so slightly, so as to spill the wind from their underside, as a skipper slacks sheets to deaden his boat's headway, and the wonderful upward spiral flight began.

Just how he does it only the eagle himself knows; and with him it is largely a matter of slow learning. The young birds make a sad bungle of it when they try it for the first time, following the mother eagle, who swings just above and in front of them to show them how it is done.

Over me sweeps my eagle in slow, majestic circles; ever returning upon his course, yet ever higher than his last wheel, like a life with a great purpose in it; sliding evenly upward on the wind's endless stairway as it slips from under him. Without hurry, without exertion — just a twist of his wide-set wing quills, so slight that my eye can no

longer notice it — he swings upward ; while
the earth spreads wider and wider below
him, and rivers flash in the sun, like silver
ribbons, across the green forest carpet that
spreads away over mountain and valley to
the farthest horizon.

313

The Gladsome Life

Smaller and smaller grow the circles now,
till the vast spiral reaches its apex, and he
hangs there in the air, looking with quiet,
kindling eyes over Isaiah's royal land of
"farnesses," like a tiny humming bird poised
over the earth's great flower cup. So high
is he that one must think he glances over
the brim of things, and sees our earth as a
great bubble floating in the blue ether, with
nothing whatever below it and only himself
above. And there he stays, floating, balancing, swaying in the purring currents of
air that hold him fast in their soft arms
and brush his great wings tenderly with a
caress that never grows weary, like a great,
strong mother holding her little child.

He had fed ; he had drunk to the full from
a mountain spring. Now he rested over the

314

The
Gladsome
Life

world that nourished him and his little ones, with his keen eyes growing sleepy, and never a thought of harm to himself or any creature within his breast. For that is a splendid thing about all great creatures, even the fiercest of them : they are never cruel. They take only what they must to supply their necessities. When their wants are satisfied there is truce which they never break. They live at peace with all things, small and great, and, in their dumb unconscious way, answer to the deep harmony of the world which underlies all its superficial discords, as the music of the sea is never heard till one moves far away from the uproar along the shore.

The little wild things all know this perfectly. When an eagle, or any other bird or beast of prey, is not hunting —which is nine tenths of the time — the timidest and most defenseless creature has no fear of him whatever.

My eyes grow weary, at last, watching the noble bird, so small a speck on the infinite blue background; and they blur suddenly, thinking of the joy of his great free life, and the sadness of our unnatural humanity.

As I seek the pool again, and rest my eyes on the soft, glimmering, color-washed surface, there is a stir in the still water at my feet. Life is here too; and joy belongs, not only to the heavens, but to the earth as well. A long twig from a fallen tree had thrust itself deep into the stream; its outer end swayed, and rose and fell rhythmically in the current. While I was watching the eagle a little turtle found the twig and laid himself across it, one flipper clinched into a knot to hold him steady, the others hanging listlessly and swinging to keep the balance perfect as he teetered up and down, up and down, with the great, purring river to do his work for him and join his silent play. And there he lay for half the morning — as long as I stayed to watch him — swinging, swaying, rising, falling, glad of his little life, which was yet big enough to know pleasure, glad of light and motion, and,

The Gladsome Life

316

The Gladsome Life

for aught I know, glad of a music in the stream below, the faint echo of the rustling, rippling, fluting music that filled the air and the woods all around me.

Life is a glad thing for the wood folk; that is what the great eagle was saying, far overhead; that is what the little turtle said, swaying up and down on his twig at my feet; that is what every singing bird and leaping salmon said, and every piping frog along the shore, and every insect buzzing about my ears in the warm sunshine. I remembered suddenly a curious fact, which till then had never come home to me with its true significance: in all my years of watching the wild things — watching, not to record, or to make a story, but only to see and understand for myself just what they were doing, and what they thought and felt — I had never yet met an unhappy bird or animal. Nor have I ever met one, before or since, in whom the dominant note was not gladness of living. I have met all sorts and conditions of beasts and birds at close quarters; some whose whole nature seemed bent into a question mark, like certain jays and turkeys and deer, and one moose that I could not keep away from my camp for any length of time; some fond, like a certain big green frog that attached himself to me with an affection that denied his cold blood; some foolish, like the fawn that would never follow his leader; some morose and ugly, like the big bull moose that first watched and then tried twice to kill me; but never a one, great or small, among them all, to whom life did not seem to offer a brimming cup, and who did not, even in times of danger and want, rejoice in his powers and live gladly, with an utter absence of that worry and anxiety which make wreck of our human life.

I stood by a runway in the big woods one morning, watching for a deer that dogs were driving. From the lake I had listened to the whole story,— the first eager, sniffing yelps, the sharp, clear note that meant a fresh track, and then the deep-lunged, savage chorus sweeping up the ridge, which told of a deer afoot and running for his life. I knew something of the deer's habits in that region; knew also that the hunters were over the ridge, watching by a lake that the deer had deserted weeks ago; and so I headed for a favorite runway, to let the deer slip by me and to club the dogs away as they came on. For deer hounding and deer coursing are detestable sports, whether the law allow them or not, and whether the dogs be mongrel curs that follow their noses or imported greyhounds with a pedigree that run by sight, followed by a field of thoroughbreds.

On the way to the runway a curious thing happened. A big hawk swooped into some berry bushes ahead of me with strong, even slant, and rose in a moment with the unmistakable air of disappointment showing all over him, from beak to tail tip. I stole up to the bushes cautiously to find out what he was after, and to match my eyes with his. There I saw, first one, then five or six

well-grown young partridges crouched in
their hiding places among the brown leaves,
rejoicing apparently in the wonderful coloring which Nature gave them, and in their
own power, learned from their mother, to lie
still and so be safe till danger passed. There
was no fear manifest whatever; no shadow
of anxiety for any foolish youngster who
might turn his head and so let the hawk see
him. In a moment they were all gliding
away with soft, inquisitive *kwit-kwits*, turning their heads to eye me curiously, and
anon picking up the dried berries that lay
about plentifully. Among them all there
was no trace of a thought for the hawk that
had just swooped. And why should there
be? Had they not just fooled him perfectly,
and were not their eyes as keen to do it
again when the need should come?

I was thinking about it, wondering at this
strange kind of fear that is merely watchful,
with no trace of our terror or anxiety for the
future in it, when twigs began to crackle and a
big buck came bounding down the runway.

319
*The Gladsome
Life*

320

The
Gladsome
Life

Near me he stopped and turned to listen, shaking his antlers indignantly, and stamping his fore foot hard at such an uproar in his quiet woods. He trotted past me, his great muscles working like well oiled machinery under his velvet coat; then, instead of keeping on to water, he leaped over a windfall — a magnificent exhibition of power, taken as gracefully as if he were but playing — and dashed away through the swamp, to kill the scent of his flying feet.

An hour or two later I saw him enter the lake quietly from another runway and swim across with deep, powerful strokes. On the farther shore he stopped a moment to shake himself and to listen to the far-away cry of the hounds. He had run as much as he wished, to stretch his big muscles, and was indisposed now to run farther and tire himself, when he could so easily get rid of the noisy pack. But there was no terror in the shake of his antlers, nor in the angry

stamp of his fore foot, and no sense save that
of conscious power and ability to take care of
himself in the mighty bounds that lifted him
like a bird over the windfalls into the shelter
and silence of the big woods.

At times, I know, it happens differently,
when a deer is fairly run down and killed
by dogs or wolves; but though I have seen
them dog-driven many times, and once when
the great gray timber wolves were running
their trail, I have never yet seen a deer lose
his perfect confidence in himself, and his
splendid sense of superiority over those that
follow him. Once, in deep snow, I saved a
deer's life just as the dogs were closing in
on him; but up to the moment when he
gave his last bound and laid his head down
quietly on the crust to rest, I saw no evidence whatever of the wild terrors and
frightful excitement that we have attributed
to driven creatures.

The same is true of foxes, and even of
rabbits. The weak and foolish die young,
under the talon or paw of stronger creatures.

321

The Gladsome Life

The rest have escaped so often, played and run so systematically till every nerve and muscle is trained to its perfect work, that they seem to have no thought whatever that the last danger may have its triumph.

Watch the dogs yonder, driving a fox through the winter woods. Their feet, cut by briers and crust, leave red trails over the snow; their tails have all bloody stumps, where the ends have been whipped off in frantic wagging. You cannot call, you can scarcely club them from the trail. They seem half crazy, half hypnotized by the scent in their noses. Their wild cry, especially if you be near them, is almost painful in its intensity as they run blindly through the woods. And it makes no difference to them, apparently, whether they get their fox or not. If he is shot before them, they sniff the body, wondering for a moment; then they roll in the snow and go off to find another trail. If the fox runs all day, as usual, they follow till footsore and weary; then sleep awhile, and come limping home in the morning.

"TROTS TO THE BROOK AND JUMPS
FROM STONE TO STONE"

Now cut ahead of the dogs to the runway and watch for the fox. Here is the hunted creature. He comes loping along, light as a wind-blown feather, his brush floating out like a great plume behind him. He stops to listen to his heavy-footed pursuers, capers a bit in self-satisfaction, chases his tail if he is a young fox, makes a crisscross of tracks, trots to the brook and jumps from stone to stone; then he makes his way thoughtfully over dry places, which hold no scent, to the top of the ridge, where he can locate the danger perfectly, and curls himself up on a warm rock and takes a nap. When the cry comes too near he slips down on the other side of the ridge, where the breeze seems to blow him away to the next hill.

There are exceptions here too; exceptions that only prove the great rule of gladness in animal life, even when we would expect wild terrors. Of scores of foxes that have passed under my eyes, with a savage hunting cry behind them, I have never seen but one that did not give the impression of getting far more fun out of it than the dogs that were driving him. And that is why he so rarely takes to earth, where he could so easily and simply escape it all, if he chose. When the weather is fine he keeps to his legs all day; but when the going is heavy, or his tail gets wet in mushy snow, he runs awhile to stretch his muscles, then slips into a den and lies down in peace. Let dogs bark; the ground is frozen, and they cannot scratch him out.

I have written these three things, of partridge and deer and fox — while twenty others come bubbling up to remembrance that one need not write — simply to suggest the great fact, so evident among all wild creatures, — from the tiniest warbler, lifting his sweet song to the sunrise amid a hundred enemies, to the great eagle, resting safe in air a thousand feet above the highest mountain peak; and from the little wood mouse, pushing his snow tunnels bravely under the very feet of hungry fox and wild-cat, to the great moose, breasting down a birch tree to feed on its top when maple and wicopy twigs are buried deep

under the northern snows, — that life is a glad thing to Nature's children, so glad that cold cannot chill, nor danger overwhelm, nor even hunger deaden its gladness. I have seen deer, gaunt as pictures from an Indian famine district, so poor that all their ribs showed like barrel hoops across their collapsed sides; yet the yearlings played together as they wandered in their search for food through the bare, hungry woods. And I have stood on the edge of the desolate northern barrens when the icy blasts roared over them and all comfort seemed buried so deep that only the advice of Job's wife seemed pertinent: to "curse God and die." And lo! in the midst of blasphemy, the flutter of tiny wings, light and laughter of little bright eyes, chatter of chickadees calling each other cheerily as they hunted the ice-bound twigs over and over for the morsel that Nature had hidden there, somewhere, in the fat autumn days; and then one clear, sweet love note, as if an angel had blown a little flute, tinkling over the bleak desolation

327

The Gladsome Life

328

The Gladsome Life

to tell me that spring was coming, and that even here, meanwhile, life was well worth the living.

The fact is, Nature takes care of her creatures so well — gives them food without care, soft colors to hide, and nimble legs to run away with — that, so far as I have ever observed, they seldom have a thought in their heads for anything but the plain comfort and gladness of living.

It is only when one looks at the animal from above, studies him psychologically for a moment, and remembers what wonderful provision Nature has made to keep him from all the evils of anxious forethought, that one can understand this gladness.

In the first place, he has no such pains as we are accustomed to find in ourselves and sympathize with in our neighbors. Three fourths, at least, of all our pain is mental; is born of an overwrought nervous organization, or imagination. If our pains were only those that actually exist in our legs or backs, we

could worry along very well to a good old
age, as the bears and squirrels do.   For the
animal has no great mentality, certainly
not enough to triple his pains thereby, and
no imagination whatever to bother him.
Your Christian-Science friend would find
him a slippery subject, smooth and difficult
as the dome of the Statehouse to get a grip
upon.   When he is sick he knows it, and
goes to sleep sensibly; when he is well he
needs no faith to assure him of the fact.   He
has his pains, to be sure, but they are only
those in his legs and back; and even here
the nervous organization is much coarser
than ours, and the pain less severe.   He has
also a most excellent and wholesome disposition to make as little, not as much, of his
pains as possible.

I have noticed a score of times in han-
dling wounded animals that, when once I
have won their confidence so that they
have no fear of my hurting them willfully,
they let me bind up their wounds and twist
the broken bones into place, and even cut

The
Gladsome
Life

away the flesh; and they show almost no evidence of suffering. That their pain is very slight compared with ours is absolutely certain.

I have sometimes found animals in the woods, bruised, wounded, bleeding, from some of the savage battles that they wage among themselves in the mating season. The first thought, naturally, is how keenly they must suffer as the ugly wounds grow cold. Now comes Nature, the wise physician. In ten minutes she has them well in hand. They sink into a dozy, dreamy slumber, as free from pain or care as an opium smoker. And there they stay, for hours or days, under the soft anæsthetic until ready to range the woods for food again, or till death comes gently and puts them to sleep.

I have watched animals stricken sore by a bullet, feeding or resting quietly; have noted little trout with half their jaws torn away rising freely to the same fly that injured them; have watched a muskrat cutting his own leg off with his teeth to free himself from the trap that held him (all unwillingly, Gentle Reader ; for I hate such things, as you do), but I have never yet seen an animal that seemed to suffer a hundredth part of the pain that an ordinary man would suffer under the same circumstances.

Children suffer far less than their elders with the same disease, and savage races less than civilized ones ; all of which points far down to the animal that, with none of our mentality or imagination or tense-strung nervous organization, escapes largely our aches and pains. This is only one more of Nature's wise ways, in withholding pain mostly from those least able to endure it.

Of purely mental sufferings the animal has but one, the grief which comes from loss of the young or the mate. In this we have read only of the exceptional cases, — the rarely exceptional, — tinctured also with the inevitable human imagination, and so have come to accept grossly exaggerated conceptions of animal grief.

The
Gladsome
Life

A mother bird's nest is destroyed. The storm beats it down; or the black snake lays his coils around it; or the small boy robs it thoughtlessly; or the professional egg-collector, whose name and whose business be anathema, puts it into his box of abominations. The mother bird haunts the spot a few hours, — rarely longer than that, — then glides away into deeper solitudes. In a few days she has another nest, and is brooding eggs more wisely hidden. This is the great rule, not the exception, of the gladsome bird life. Happy for them and for us that it is so; else, instead of the glorious morning chorus, the woods would be filled always with lamentations.

When the young birds or animals are taken away, or killed by hungry prowlers, the mother's grief endures a little longer. But even here Nature is kind. The mother love for helpless little ones, which makes the summer wilderness such a wonderful place to open one's eyes in, is but a temporary instinct. At best it endures but a few weeks, after which the little ones go away to take care of themselves, and the mother lets them go gladly, thinking that now she can lay on fat for herself against the cold winter.

If the time be yet seasonable when accident befalls, the mother wastes but few hours in useless mourning. She makes a new nest, or hollows out a better den, or drops her young in deeper seclusion, and forgets the loss, speedily and absolutely, in rearing and teaching the new brood,—hurrying the process and taking less care, because the time is short. It is a noteworthy fact— you can see it for yourself any late summer in the woods—that these late-coming offspring are less cared for than the earlier. The mother must have a certain period of leisure for herself to get ready for winter, and she takes it, usually, whether the young are fully prepared for life or not. It is from these second broods largely that birds and beasts of prey keep themselves alive during times of hunger and scarcity.

333

The Gladsome Life

334

The
Gladsome
Life

They are less carefully taught, and so are caught more easily. This again is not the exception, but the great rule of animal life.

And this is another of Mother Nature's wise ways. She must care for the deer and partridge; but she must also remember the owl and the panther that cry out to her in their hunger. And how could she accomplish that miracle of contradiction without exciting our hate and utter abhorrence, if she gave to her wild creatures the human griefs and pains with which they are so often endowed by our sensitive imagination?

Of these small griefs and pains, such as they are, the mothers alone are the inheritors. The male birds and animals, almost without exception so far as I have observed, have no griefs, but rather welcome the loss of the young. This is partly because it leaves them free to shift and feed for themselves — your male animal is essentially a selfish and happy creature — and partly because it opens to them anew the joys of winning their mates over again.

The second great reason for the gladness of animal life is that the animal has no fears. The widespread animal fear, which is indeed the salvation of all the little wild things, is so utterly different from our "faithless fears and worldly anxieties" that another name — watchfulness, perhaps, or timidity, or distrust — should be given to it in strict truth.

This animal fear, be it remembered, is not so much an instinctive thing as a plain matter of teaching. Indeed, inquisitiveness is a much stronger trait of all animals than fear. The world is so full of things the animal does not understand that he is always agog to find out a little more.

I was sitting on a stump one day in the woods, plucking some partridges for my dinner. A slight motion in the underbrush roused me from my absorption; and there was a big bull moose, half hid in the dwarf spruces, watching me and the fluttering feathers, with wonder and intense curiosity written all over his ugly black face. And I have caught bear and deer and crows and

335

The Gladsome Life

squirrels and little wood warblers at the same inquisitive game, again and again. If you sit down in the woods anywhere, and do any queer or simple thing you will, the time will not be long before you find shy bright eyes, all round with wonder, watching you with delicious little waverings between the timidity which urges them away and the curiosity which always brings them back again, if you but know how to keep still and disguise your interest.

If you find a young bird or animal, in nest or den, young enough so that the mother's example has not yet produced its effect, you will probably note only two instincts. The first and greatest instinct, that of obedience, is not for you to command; though you may get some strong hints of it, if you approach silently and utter some low, cautious sound in imitation of the mother creature. The two which you may surely find are: the instinct to eat, and the instinct to lie still and let nature's coloring do its good work of hiding. (There is another reason for quietness: a bird — and, to a less extent, an animal — gives forth no scent when he is still and his pores are closed. He lies quiet to escape the nose as well as the eyes of his enemy. That, however, is another matter.) But you will find no fear there. The little thing will feed from your hand as readily as from its mother, if you catch him soon enough.

Afterwards come the lessons of watchfulness and timidity, which we have called fear, — to sort the sounds and sights and smells of the woods, and to act accordingly; now to lie still, and now to bristle your pinfeathers, so as to look big and scare an intruder; now to hiss, or growl, or scratch, or cry out for your mother; and now, at last, to dive for cover or take to your legs in a straightaway run, — all of which are learned, not by instinct, but by teaching and example.

And these are not fears at all, in our sense of the word, but rules of conduct; as a car horse stops when the bell jingles; as a man

337

The Gladsome Life

The Gladsome Life

turns to the right, because he has learned to do so, or bends forward in running, or jumps forward when he hears an unknown noise close behind him.

To make a rough and of course inadequate generalization, all our human fears arise from three great sources : the thought of pain or bodily harm, the thought of future calamity, and the thought of death. Now Nature in mercy has kept all these things from the wild creatures, who have no way of making provision against them, nor any capacity for faith, by which alone such fears are overcome.

First, in the matter of bodily harm or pain : The animal has lived a natural life and, as a rule, knows no pain whatever. He likewise has never been harmed by any creature — except perhaps an occasional nip by his mother, to teach him obedience. So he runs or flies through the big woods without any thought of the pains that he has never felt and does not know.

Neither does any thought of future calamity bother his little head, for he knows no calamity and no future. I am not speaking now of what we know, or think we know, concerning the animal's future; but only of what he knows, and what he knows he knows. With the exception of the few wild creatures that lay up stores for winter — and they are the happiest — he lives wholly in the present. He feels well; his eyes are keen and his muscles ready; he has enough, or expects enough at the next turn of the trail. And that is his wisdom of experience.

As for death, that is forever out of the animal's thinking. Not one in a thousand creatures ever sees death — except, of course, the insects or other wild things that they eat, and these are not death but good food, as we regard a beefsteak. If they do see it, they pass it by suspiciously, like a tent, or a canoe, or any other thing which they do not understand, and which they have not been taught by their mothers how to meet. Scores of times I have watched birds and animals by their own dead mates or little ones. Until the thing grows cold they treat

339

The Gladsome Life

The Gladsome Life

it as if it were sleeping. Then they grow suspicious, look at the body strangely, sniff it at a distance, never touching it with their noses. They glide away at last, wondering why it is so cold, why it does not move or come when it is called. Then, circling through the underbrush, you will hear them calling and searching elsewhere for the little one that they have just left.

So far as I know, the ants, some tribes of which bury their dead, and the bees, which kill their drones at the proper season, are the only possible exception to this general rule of animal life. And these little creatures are too unknown, too mysterious, too contradictory a mixture of dense stupidity and profound wisdom to allow a positive theory as to how clearly they think, how blindly they are instinctive, or how far they are conscious of the meaning of what they do daily all their lives.

Bodily harm, future calamity, death,— these three things can never enter consciously into the animal's head; and there is nothing in his experience to clothe the last great enemy, or friend, with any meaning. Therefore are they glad, being mercifully delivered from the bondage of our fears.

I am still sitting on the old log by the salmon pool, with the great river purring by and the white foam patches floating down from the riffles. A second little turtle has joined the first on his teeter board; they are swinging up and down, up and down, in the kindly current together. The river is full of insect life below them; they will eat when they get ready. Meanwhile they swing and enjoy their little life. Far over the mountain soars the great eagle, resting on the winds. The earth has food and drink below; he will come down when he is hungry. Meanwhile he looks down over the brim of things and is satisfied. The birds have not yet hushed their morning song in the woods behind me; too happy to eat, they must sing a little longer. Where the pool dimples and rolls lazily the salmon are leaping in

The Gladsome Life

their strength; frogs pipe and blink on the lily pads riding at anchor; and over their heads in the flood of sunshine buzz the myriads of little things that cannot be still for gladness. Nature above and below tingles with the joy of mere living — a joy that bubbles over, like a spring, so that all who will, even of the race of men who have lost or forgotten their birthright, may come back and drink of its abundance and be satisfied.

How the Animals Die

How the Animals Die

THE scream of an eagle — a rare sound in the summer wilderness — brought me hurrying out of my *commoosie* to know what had caused Cheplahgan to break the silence. He was poised over his mountain top at an enormous altitude, wheeling in small erratic circles, like an eaglet learning to use the wind under his broad wings, and anon sending his wild cry out over the startled woods.

Clearly something was wrong with Cheplahgan. This was no eaglet calling aloud to his unknown mate, or trying for the first time the eagle's wonderful spiral flight; neither was it one of a pair of the royal birds that I had been watching and following for weeks,

345

whose nest and little ones I had found at last on a distant crag. Occasionally, as I followed them, I had glimpses of another eagle, a huge, solitary old fellow without a mate, whose life had been a puzzle and a mystery to me all summer. It was he who was now crying aloud over the high mountain, where I had often seen him looking out with quiet eyes over the wide splendid domain that he ruled no longer, but had given over to younger eagles—his nestlings, perhaps— only claiming for himself the right to stay and hunt where he and his vanished mate had so long held sway. For most birds and beasts of prey have their own hunting grounds; and, until they give them up, none other goes a-poaching there. It was this that had chiefly puzzled me all summer. Now I ran to a point and sat down quietly against a weatherworn root that blended with the gray of my jacket, and focused my glasses steadily on Cheplahgan to see what he would do.

Soon the erratic circles narrowed to a center, about which the great eagle turned as on a pivot; the wild cry was hushed, and he spread his wings wide and stiff, as an eagle does when resting on the air. For several minutes I could see no motion; he seemed just a tiny dark line drawn across the infinite blue background. Then the line grew longer, heavier; and I knew that he was coming down straight towards me.

Lower and lower he came, slanting slowly down in a long incline by imperceptible degrees, without a quiver of his wide-set wings. Lower still and nearer, till I saw with wonder that his head, instead of being carried eagle fashion, in a perfect line with body and tail, drooped forward as if it were heavy. Straight over the point he sailed, so near that I heard the faint crackle of his pinions, like the rustle of heavy silk. The head drooped lower still; the fierce, wild eyes were half closed as he passed. Only once did he veer slightly, to escape a tall stub that thrust its naked bulk above the woods athwart his path. Then with rigid wings he crossed the bay below the point, still slanting

347

How the Animals Die

gently down to earth, and vanished silently into the drooping arms of the dark woods beyond.

Clearly something was wrong with Cheplahgan. Such an eagle's flight was never seen before. I marked the spot where he disappeared, between two giant trees, and followed swiftly in my canoe. Just within the fringe of forest I found him, resting peacefully for the first time on mother earth, his head lying across the moss-cushioned root of an old cedar, his wings outstretched among the cool green ferns — dead.

Behind my tent in the wilderness, last summer, was a little spring. I used to go there often, not to drink, but just to sit beside it awhile and grow quiet, watching its cool waters bubble up out of the dark earth amid dancing pebbles to steal away among the ferns and mosses on its errand of unchanging mercy. Now and then, as I watched, the little wild things would hear the low tinkle of invitation to all who were athirst,

"A LITTLE WOOD WARBLER WAS SITTING
ON A FROND OF EVERGREEN"

and would come swiftly to drink. Seeing me they would draw back among the ferns to watch and listen; but the little rivulet tinkled away unchanged, and they always came back at last, taking me shyly for their friend because I sat beside their spring.

One day when I came a little wood warbler was sitting on a frond of evergreen that hung over the spring as if to protect it. For several days I had noticed him there, resting or flitting silently about the underbrush. He rarely drank, but seemed to be there, as I was, just because he loved the place. He was old and alone; the dark feathers of his head were streaked with gray, and his feet showed the wrinkled scales that age always brings to the birds. As if he had learned the gentleness of age, he seemed to have no fear, barely moving aside as I approached, and at times coming close beside me as I looked into his spring. To-day he was quieter than usual; when I stretched out my hand to take him he made no resistance, but settled down quietly on my finger and closed his eyes.

352

How the
Animals Die

For a half hour or more he sat there contentedly, blinking sleepily now and then, and opening his eyes wide when I brought him a drop of water on the tip of my finger. As twilight came on, and all the voices of the wood were hushed, I put him back on the evergreen frond, where he nodded off to sleep before I went away.

Next morning he was closer to the friendly spring, on a lower branch of the big evergreen. Again he nestled down in my hand and drank gratefully the drop from my finger tip. At twilight I found him hanging head down from a spruce root, his feet clinched in a hold that would never loosen, his bill just touching the life-giving water. He had fallen asleep there, in peace, by the spring that he had known and loved all his life, and whose waters welled up to his lips and held his image in their heart to the last moment.

How do the animals die? — quietly, peacefully, nine tenths of them, as the eagle died in his own free element, and the little wood warbler by the spring he loved. For these two are but types of the death that goes on in the woods continually. The only exception is in this: that they were seen by too inquisitive eyes. The vast majority steal away into the solitudes they love and lay them down unseen, where the leaves shall presently cover them from the sight of friends and enemies alike.

353

How the Animals Die

We rarely discover them at such times, for the instinct of the animal is to go away as far as possible into the deepest coverts. We see only the exceptional cases, the quail in the hawk's grip, the squirrel limp and quiet under the paw of cat or weasel; but the unnumbered multitudes that choose their own place and close their eyes for the last time, as peacefully as ever they lay down to sleep, are hidden from our sight.

There is a curious animal trait which may account for this, and also explain why we have such curious, foolish conceptions of animal death as a tragic, violent thing. All animals and birds have a strong distrust and

354

How the Animals Die

antipathy for any queerness or irregularity among their own kind. Except in rare cases, no animals or birds will tolerate any cripple or deformed or sickly member among them. They set upon him fiercely and drive him away. So when an animal, grown old and feeble, feels the queerness of some new thing stealing upon him he slips away, in obedience to a law of protection that he has noted all his life, and, knowing no such thing as death, thinks he is but escaping discomfort when he lies down in hiding for the last time.

A score of times, with both wild and domestic animals, I have watched this and wondered. Sometimes it is entirely unconscious, as with an old bear that I found one summer, who had laid him down for his winter sleep under a root, as usual, but did not waken when the snows were gone and the spring sun called him cheerily. Sometimes it is a triumphant sense of cunning, as with certain ducks that, when wounded, dive and grasp a root under water, and die there,

thinking how perfectly they escape their
enemies. Sometimes it is a faint, unknown
instinct that calls them they know not
whither, as with the caribou, many of whom
go far away to a spot they have never seen,
where generations of their ancestors have
preceded them, and there lie down with the
larches swaying above them gently, wondering why they are so sleepy, and why they care
not for good moss and water. And sometimes
it is but a blind impulse to get away, as many
birds fly straight out to sea, till they can go
no farther, and fold their tired wings and sleep
ere the ocean touches them.

*How the
Animals Die*

One day you may see your canary fluttering his unused wings ceaselessly against the
bars of his cage, where he lived so long content. Were you wise, you would open the
door; for a call, stronger far than your artificial relations, is bidding him come, — the
call of his forgotten ancestors. Next day he
lies dead on the floor of his cage, and there
is left for him only a burial more artificial
than his poor life.

356

How the Animals Die

"But," some reader objects, "what about the catastrophes, the tragedies?" There may be a few, possibly, if you see with your imagination rather than with your eyes; but they are rarer far than human catastrophes. And as the vast majority of mankind die, not by earthquake or famine, but peacefully on their beds, so the vast majority of wild creatures die quietly in beds of their own choosing. Except where man steps in and interferes with the natural order of things, or brutally kills a brooding or nursing mother, Nature knows no tragedies. A partridge falls under the owl's swoop. That is bad for the partridge, — who is, however, almost invariably one of the weak or foolish ones who have not learned to be obedient with his brethren, — but there are two young owls up in the tree-top yonder, who will rejoice and be glad at the good dinner brought home to them by a careful and loving mother.

As a rule Nature, as well as man, protects her brooding mothers, on whom helpless lives depend, with infinite care and cunning. Even the fox cannot smell them at such times, though he pass close by. But should the mother fall — even here we have let our human imagination run away with us — the young do not starve to death, as we imagine pitifully. They cry out for their dinner; the mother is not near to hush them, to tell them that silence is the law of the woods for help-less things. They cry again; the crow or the weasel hears, and there is a speedy end to the family without delay or suffering. This is the way of the woods.

There are violent deaths, to be sure; but these are usually the most painless and mer-ciful. A deer goes down under the spring of a panther watching above the runways. We imagine that to be a fearful death, and painters have depicted it in the colors of agony. As a matter of fact, there is prob-ably no pain whatever. Livingstone, who lay under the paw of a lion with his shoulder crushed and his arm gashed with seams whose scars he carried to his grave, felt no pain and did not even know that he was

358

How the Animals Die

hurt. He was the first to call attention to the fact that the rush and spring of a savage animal brings a kind of merciful numbness that kills pain perfectly, and seems also to take away all feeling and volition; so that one is glad simply to lie still — his only hope, by the way, if he is to escape. If this is true of men, it is ten times more so of the animals, which have none of our nervousness or imagination.

There are many other things which point to the same comfortable conclusion. Soldiers in the rush of a charge or the run of a retreat are often mortally hurt without knowing it till they faint and fall an hour later. Every one has seen a mouse under the cat's paw, and a toad in the jaws of a snake, and knows that, so far as the stricken creatures are concerned, there is no suggestion there of death or suffering. And I have seen larger creatures — rabbits and grouse and deer — lying passive under the talon or claw that crushed them, and could only wonder at Nature's mercifulness. Death was not hard, but kind,

and covered over with a vague unreality that hid all meaning from the animals' eyes and made them wonder what was happening.

Sometimes the animals die of cold. I have occasionally found, on bitter mornings, owls and crows and little birds hanging each by one claw to a branch, dead and frozen. That is also a merciful and painless ending. I have been lost in the woods in winter. I have felt the delicious languor of the cold, the soft infolding arms of the snow that beckoned restfully as twilight fell, when the hush was on the woods and human muscles could act no longer. And that is a gentle way to die when the time comes.

Sometimes the animals die of hunger, when an ice storm covers all their feeding grounds. That also, as any one knows who has gone days without food, is far more merciful than any sickness. Long before pain comes, a dozy lassitude blunts the edge of all feeling. Sometimes it is fire or flood; but in that case the creature runs away, with the confidence that he always feels in his legs or wings, till

359

How the Animals Die

360

How the
Animals Die

the end comes swift and sure. Those that escape huddle together in the safe spots, forgetting natural enmities and all things else save a great wonder at what has come to pass. In short, unless the animals are to live always and become a nuisance or a danger by their increase, Nature is kind, even in her sterner moods, in taking care that death comes to all her creatures without pain or terror. And what is true of the animals was true of man till he sought out many inventions to make sickness intolerable and death an enemy.

All these latter cases, it is well to remember, are the striking variations, not the rule of the woods. The vast majority of animals go away quietly when their time comes; and their death is not recorded because man has eyes only for exceptions. He desires a miracle, but overlooks the sunsets. Something calls the creature away from his daily round; age or natural disease touches him gently in a way that he has not felt before. He steals away, obeying the old warning instinct of his kind, and picks out a spot where they shall not find him till he is well again. The brook sings on its way to the sea; the waters lap and tinkle on the pebbles as the breeze rocks them; the wind is crooning in the pines, — the old, sweet lullaby that he heard when his ears first opened to the harmony of the world. The shadows lengthen; the twilight deepens; his eyes grow drowsy; he falls asleep. And his last conscious thought, since he knows no death, is that he will waken in the morning when the light calls him.

361

*How the
Animals Die*

GLOSSARY OF INDIAN NAMES

Cheokhes, *chē-ok-hĕs',* the mink.

Cheplahgan, *chep-lăh'gan,* the bald eagle.

Ch'geegee-lokh-sis, *ch'gee-gee'lock-sis,* the chickadee.

Chigwooltz, *chig-wooltz',* the bullfrog.

Clóte Scarpe, a legendary hero, like Hiawatha, of the Northern Indians. Pronounced variously, Clote Scarpe, Groscap, Gluscap, etc.

Commoosie, *com-moo-sie',* a little shelter, or hut, of boughs and bark.

Deedeeaskh, *dee-dee'ask,* the blue jay.

Eleemos, *el-ee'mos,* the fox.

Hawahak, *hă-wă-hăk',* the hawk.

Hukweem, *huk-weem',* the great northern diver, or loon.

Ismaques, *iss-mă-ques',* the fishhawk.

Kagax, *kăg'ăx,* the weasel.

Kakagos, *kă-kă-gŏs',* the raven.

K'dunk, *k'dunk',* the toad.

Keeokuskh, *kee-o-kusk',* the muskrat.

Keeonekh, *kee'o-nek,* the otter.

Killooleet, *kil'loo-leet',* the white-throated sparrow.

Kookooskoos, *koo-koo-skoos',* the great horned owl.

Koskomenos, *kŏs'kŏm-e-nŏs',* the kingfisher.

Kupkawis, *cup-ka'wis,* the barred owl.

Kwaseekho, *kwâ-seek'ho,* the sheldrake.

Lhoks, *locks,* the panther.

Malsun, *măl'sun,* the wolf.

Meeko, *meek'ō,* the red squirrel.

Megaleep, *meg'â-leep,* the caribou.

Milicete, *mil'ĭ-cete,* the name of an Indian tribe; written also Malicete.

Mitches, *mit'chĕs,* the birch partridge, or ruffed grouse.

Moktaques, *mok-tâ'ques,* the hare.

Mooween, *moo-ween',* the black bear.

Musquash, *mus'quâsh,* the muskrat.

Nemox, *nĕm'ox,* the fisher.

Pekquam, *pek-wăm',* the fisher.

Quoskh, *quoskh,* the blue heron.

Seksagadagee, *sek'sâ-gā-dâ'gee,* the Canada grouse, or spruce partridge.

Skooktum, *skook'tum,* the trout.

Tookhees, *tôk'hees,* the wood mouse.

Umquenawis, *um-que-nâ'wis,* the moose.

Unk Wunk, *unk' wunk,* the porcupine.

Upweekis, *up-week'iss,* the Canada lynx.